INTRODUCTION

Turkey is a large country in the shape of a rectangle - the only country bordered by four seas: the Mediterranean, the Aegean, the Black Sea and the Sea of Marmara, the smallest sea in the world. Teeming with fish, it belongs solely to Turkey where it is known as the "sweet sea".

The country's size is such that it takes seventy-five minutes for the sun to rise on all sixty-seven provinces. Turkey is a glorious, fascinating country, a perpetual divide between West and East, the past and the present, secularism and Islam, and between conservation and progress.

The natural beauty of the landscape, from the steep mountains in the interior to the undulating steppe, from the lunar landscapes of Cappadocia to the translucent seas, from the pebble and sandy beaches to the remains of ancient temples and other traces of the past, all make this a most enchanting country. Herodotus, who was born here, said that the Turkish coast and sky were the most beautiful in the world. It is a country where over the centuries twelve civilisations have taken root, each one building on the former, and where each one has left its mark giving shape and origin to an immense culture of which we are all, at least in part, children and heirs.

After Palestine, it is the country where Christians can rediscover the origins of their faith, - the source of both the Tigris and Euphrates, the biblical rivers of Paradise and the progenitors of humanity.

Turkey is also a country described in art and literature as a dissolute place, where voluptuousness and sensuality ruled in the harem where the Sultan reigned over plump and ravishing odalisques. Lycian society, in Turkey, governed by a parliament, was the world's most ancient republic.

Turks are hospitable, generous and helpful. In the big cities people are frenzied and always in a hurry, but in the interior people live according to the same nomadic and peasant rules and traditions that have existed for centuries.

For nine thousand years, stretching back to the Neolithic period, women in Turkey have woven and stitched carpets; mostly Kilims which abound in religious and mythological symbols, and are called, not by chance, the "carpets of the gods". Turkish cuisine, the third most important in the world after French and Chinese, has a long tradition of giving pleasure in order, at one time, to titillate the sophisticated palates of the Sultans. Indeed the ancient Romans employed Turkish cooks to work in their kitchens.

Turkey is the paradise of the olive, the vine, citrus fruits and vegetables: it ranks sixth in the world in terms of wine production. It is the country of cashmere, the highly-prized wool, and of cotton and linen: in the south of the country vast acreages of plantations are found alongside modern oil refineries. Turkey is a country with fifty-seven million inhabitants, and it has been a republic since 1923 when Ankara became the capital.

This great city is modern, accessible and filled with tree-lined boulevards. It is also a European political city and the seat of parliament.

But Istanbul is still the centre of ancient attractions that will never be forgotten in the souls of the Turks. Today the city looks like an old lady, with its silhouette of minarets and its long bridge, a city of magic and mystery.

It has kept its magnificent ruins of the past and the glory of a place at one time dominated by three empires, fabulous Byzantium, then Constantinople the magnificent, and today beautiful Istanbul.

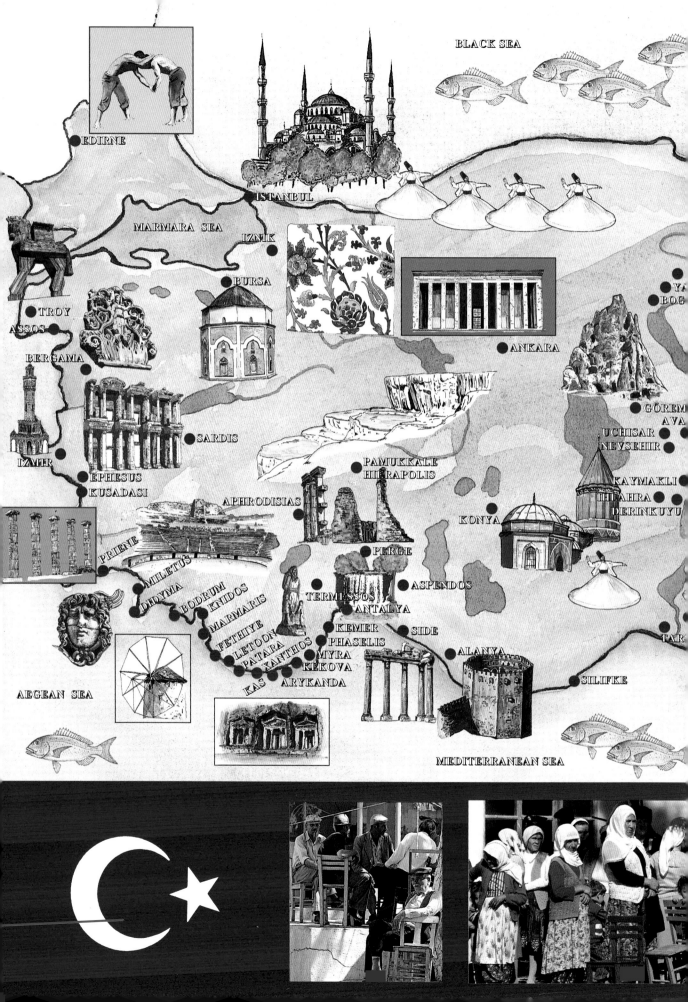

Luciana Savelli Listri

TURKEY
A COMPLETE GUIDE

KINA - BECOCCI

KESKİN
COLOR

PRODUCTION

Art director: Antonio Tassinari
Videoimpaginazione e copertina: Graficastudio, Firenze
Translation: Rupert Hodson
Filmset: Giotto, Firenze
Printed by: Kina Italia / Eurografica - Italy

KESKİN COLOR KARTPOSTALCILIK SAN. ve PAZ. A. Ş.

Merkez: Ankara Cad. N° 98   34410 Sirkeci – Istanbul   Tel. (0212) 514 17 47/48   Fax (0212) 512 09 64

Ist. Şube: Ankara Cad. Hoşağasi Işhani N° 107/36-37-38-39 Sirkeci – Istanbul   Tel. (0212) 514 17 47/48

Fax (0212) 512 09 64

Antalya Şube: Kisla Mah. N° 54 Sk. Gunaydin Apt. N° 6/B   07040 Antalya   Tel. (0242) 247 15 41

Fax (0242) 247 16 11

PHOTOGRAPHS

Archivio Casa Editrice Giusti di S. Becocci, Firenze – Archivio Kina Italia/Eurografica - Italy
Archivio Keskin Color, Istanbul – Archivio del Ministero Turco per la Cultura, Roma
G. Barone, Firenze – M. Casiraghi, Milano – N. Grifoni, Firenze; K&B News, Firenze – Massimo Listri, Firenze
The photograph on page 46 has been kindly presented by
MAGISTER TOUR
Head Office: Halaskargazi Cd. 321/2 80260 Sisli – Istanbul   Tel.: (0212) 230 00 00   Fax: (0212) 248 40 30

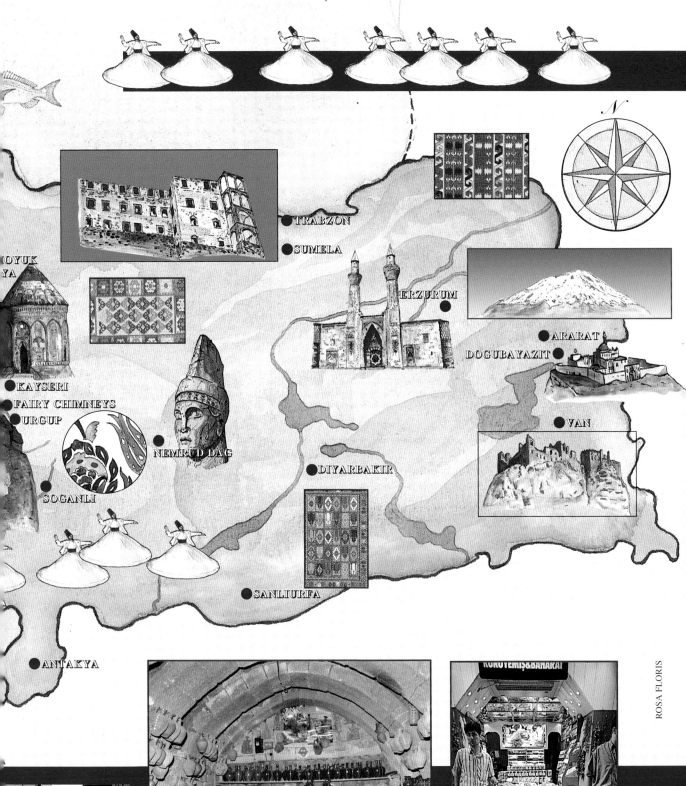

TRABZON

SUMELA

OYUK
YA

ERZURUM

ARARAT

DOGUBAYAZIT

KAYSERI

FAIRY CHIMNEYS

URGUP

VAN

NEMRUD DAG

DIYARBAKIR

SOGANLI

SANLIURFA

ANTAKYA

ROSA FLORIS

Opposite, General view of Istanbul with Santa Sophia and the Bosphorus in the background.
Above: Another view of the city with Süleyman's Mosque.

ISTANBUL

Fifteen million inhabitants coming from all kinds of races today live in what was once fabulous Byzantium before becoming Constantinople the splendid and now beautiful Istanbul. The outline of its domes, the silhouette of its minarets, the long bridge spanning the Bosphorus - the stretch of water known as the Golden Horn - all join to make this city, unique throughout the world, recognisable, mysterious and magical, built at the meeting place where two continents merge, Europe and Asia, the place where the West meets the East.

A tour of Turkey can only begin here, from this metropolis that has also been the capital of three great empires: the Roman Empire in the East, the Roman Empire of the West and the Ottoman Empire, and also where (like much of Turkey itself) many other civilisations took root. Istanbul is a vibrant and chaotic city with many different facets; it has been destroyed more than once over the centuries and many times rebuilt, struck down to rise again.

Istanbul is split by the Bosphorus (The Pass of the Ox in mythology), a narrow strait connecting the Black Sea with the Sea of Marmara, the smallest sea in the world which the Turks affectionately call the "sweet sea".

An old Turkish proverb says that whoever drinks the water from the Bosphorus even once will feel thirsty forever.

A boat trip on the Bosphorus is both suggestive and romantic. One can see the banks packed with palaces, luxurious dwellings that once belonged to great dignitaries, viziers and ambassadors, as well as the typical and colourful *Yali,* early wooden Turkish houses constructed on piles over the water.

Ortaköy, a district on the European bank, boasts a fine nineteenth-century mosque built directly underneath the bridge over the Bosphorus (Boğaziçi) and its main square is filled with shops, cafés, restaurants and book stalls. It is the intellectuals' quarter populated by artists, jugglers and street performers and it resembles Montmartre in Paris in its heyday. Ortaköy's Sunday market is noisy and cheerful, selling antiques and handicrafts.

Istanbul at dusk. In the foreground, The Galata Bridge.

Between old Istanbul and the new, the **Golden Horn**, a stretch of sea water and a natural port in the shape of a horn flows gently by; at dusk it takes on the colour of gold. The Tower of *Galata* and its legendary bridge tower over it; facing the Golden Horn is the famous **Egyptian Bazaar**, smelling sweetly of spices. The view of the Horn and of all Istanbul that can be seen from the café named after the French author Pierre Loti and constructed in perfect Turkish style is enchanting and takes one's breath away.

Another place of character is the **Çiçek Paşhai** or the passageway of flowers, filled with small restaurants where characteristic dishes can be eaten, accompanied by aniseed liqueur, *Raki*, the national drink. There an old Armenian lady with a permanently-lighted cigarette, sings sweet and heart-breaking songs accompanied by an accordion. In this corner of Istanbul, pervaded with dreamy enchantment, one feels that time stands still or that it has ceased to exist. The history of Istanbul, built on three promontories; Stanbul (on the point of the Seraglio), *Beyoğlu* and *Üsküdar*, modern Scuteri on the Asian side, began in 650 B.C.. It was traditionally thought to have been founded by Greek colonists, and in particular a certain Byzas, from whom the name Byzantium derives. Philip of Macedon attempted an invasion, but, according to legend, the goddess Hecate, whose symbols were the crescent moon and the star, saved the besieged Greeks. These same symbols, subsequently adopted by Islam, were used on the first coins minted in the city.

In 330 A.D. the city became the capital of the Roman Empire under Constantine the Great. This was the inception of Byzantine civilisation which was to last for many centuries. Palaces, churches and monuments were built and the streets adorned with statues, columns and fountains. But the city reached the height of its splendour under Justinian. It was then repeatedly invaded by Persians and Arabs, until the city entered a new era of opulence under Constantine *Porphyry*. The 11th century saw the schism between the Christian Church of the East and the Western Church; in 1204 the Crusaders sacked Constantinople; the Byzantines reconquered the city which once again attained new life. But the Ottoman Turks were not far away: on 1453 the Sultan Mahomet II brought the Byzantine Empire to an end, the city was renamed Istanbul and it became part of the Ottoman Empire. Under Süleyman the Magnificent the architect Sinan enriched it by building monuments, mosques and

Santa Sophia.

sumptuous palaces.

In 1923, with the fall of the Ottoman Empire, General Kemal Atatürk decreed the birth of the Turkish Republic, and the capital was moved to Ankara, but Istanbul remains today a centre of great attraction.

The bridge and tower of Galata

For the local people the **Bridge of Galata** is and always will be simply "the Bridge" (in spite of the fact that two others have been constructed). For a long time it was the only bridge over the Golden Horn which connected the old city with the Galata district. The ancient multi-racial quarter where Sephardic Jews, members of the Orthodox Church, Catholics, Armenians, Genoese and Venetians all lived together with their respective workshops, their markets and their offices beside the Egyptian Bazaar which dealt in perfumed coloured spices.

The modern Bridge of Galata, four hundred and sixty-eight metres long and twenty-six wide, replaced the original bridge which was destroyed by fire in 1992. Notwithstanding that, the quarter has kept its old charm, its colour and its lively working-class character, even if it

suffers from traffic congestion. It is always thronged with costermongers, small shops, and above all fishermen who offer to sell freshly caught fish which is immediately fried and served with a piece of bread: Balik Ekmek.

Still today, as in the past, every night the Galata Bridge opens and rotates to allow big ships to pass. It is dominated by the Tower of Galata, an ancient Genoese fortification sixty-eight metres high with a beautiful cone-shaped roof. Inside the tower (there are lifts) there is a gallery from which one can see the whole city of Istanbul and the view is indeed spectacular and captivating. The tower also houses a restaurant and a nightclub where every evening odalisques dressed in veils perform a belly dance for tourists, the ancient dance with such erotic overtones.

Santa Sophia

Santa Sophia, is an extraordinary religious monument. First a church, or rather a Christian sanctuary, it then became Muslim and is now a famous museum.

Santa Sophia, or *Aya Sofya* for the Muslims and *Haghia Sophia* for the Byzantines, is the great masterpiece of

Byzantine art. The church was commissioned by Justinian who chose two mathematicians, Anthemius of Tralles and Isidorus of Miletus, to plan and buid his church. Construction lasted five years and ten months, employing one handred masons and ten thousand workers. Only the finest materials were used: porphyry columns were imported from Rome and Ephesus supplied prominent architectonic elements. The icons and furnishings from all over the world.

Santa Sophia extraordinary dome collapsed following an earthquake which occurred three years after its completion. It was rebuilt by Isidorus the Younger and the church was consacreted once again by Justinian on Christmas Eve in 563 A.D.

Once inside, and positioning oneself in the middle of the central nave, one perceives the magnificence and the harmony of the building in its entirety. From this position the beauty of the dome is immediate and it seems to be utterly weightless, though it measures thirty metres in diameter, rising fifty-five metres from ground level. The interior of the dome is entirely covered with gold mosaics and the dome itself is supported by forty arches enclosing as many windows. It rests on four arched columns supported by piers. For one thousand five hundred years each of the four spandrels on the arches was decorated with an six-winged angel before Islam covered over these symbols of a different religion. Santa Sophia, thought to be the eighth wonder of the world, covers an area of seven thousand five hundred square meters. It has a central nave and two side aisles which, like the narthexes, have two storeys, with the upper storey serving as a gallery. There are one hundred and seven columns in the basilica, seventy seven of which are on the upper storey, the other forty on the ground floor. Almost all of them have splendid Byzantine capitals, decorated with carvings of acanthus leaves and bearing the monograms of **Theodora** and **Justinian** on the reverse. The famous so-called sweating column, known as the column of St. George is to be found at the north-west of the side aisle. As a result of chemical reaction with water, the column feels damp to the touch, and so was thought to have miracoulous properties.

There is a fine fourteenth-century *fragment of mosaic* of the *Deesis* (prayer and supplication) in the *Women's Gallery*; it represents *Christ Blessing with the Virgin Mary and John the Baptist* by this side. At the end of the Gallery there is another mosaic of *Christ with the Empress Zoe*, holding writings in her hand, and the Emperor Constantine IX clasping a purse of coins.

But the Basilica's most famous and important gold

A view of the extraordinary interior of Santa Sophia.

mosaic is the mosaic of Christ in the tympanum over the Imperial Gate, where the Emperor made his entrance. It portrays *Christ Pantocrator* (omnipotent) enthroned, bestowing a blessing with his right hand, and holding in his left hand an open book.

Santa Sophia has not only been damaged by earthquake and fire but it was sacked and looted in 1204 by the crusaders. On may 29 1453, when Constantinople was taken by Sultan Mehmet II, Santa Sophia was turned into a mosque, a temple of Islam. It is said that on the very afternoon of his victory, the cry of the muezzin rose for the first time in the Basilica, and the sultan went in to pray. Later four minarets were added, one of which was built of red brick and two were designed by the architect Sinan. The *Mimber* and *Mihrab* were installed, along with the eight wooden panels in the form of shields with the names of Allah, Mahomet and various Califfs.

All the mosaics, in accordance with Islamic law; were covered over with plaster and the cross was replaced by the crescent moon.

Since February 1st 1936, on the orders of Kemal Atatürk, Santa Sophia has been a Byzantine and Islamic Museum. Outside the basilica, where there was once a Baptistery, there is now a Mausoleum with the tombs of sultans and their families.

Details from the mosaics in Santa Sophia: on the right, Christ Pantocrator; below, The Emperor John II Comneno and the Empress Irene with the Virgin Mary.

A beautiful view of the Blue Mosque.

The Yerebatan Saray (Underground Palace)

The **Yerebatan Saray** was once the **Imperial Cistern**, and is a short distance from Santa Sophia and the Blue Mosque. The unobtrusive entrance opens on to a short flight of steps leading down into the Imperial Cistern wich is illuminated with coloured lighting. Three hundred and thirty six columns with Corinthian capitals support the vaulted brick roof of the Cistern, one hundred and forty metres long and seventy metres wide.

Walkways in the Cistern allow visitors to wander at will and see fish swimming in the cistern. The fish were used as an expedient to make sure that the water remained clear. This is a rather dank and murky place, but has a certain magic. The noise of incessant drops of water mingles with piped background music. At the far end there are two columns resting on bases carved with the head of Medusa apparently placed there by the Emperor Justinian's builders when the cistern was enlarged.

The Yerebatan Saray was built on the site of a Basilica, from which it takes its name.

It was built by the Emperor Constantine and altered and enlarged by Justinian between 527 and 565. Water is brought to the cistern by aqueducts built by the emperors Hadrian and Valens which supplied the Imperial Palace.

Sultan Ahmet Camii (the Blue Mosque)

The **Sultan Ahmet Camii** or **Blue Mosque** is in front of Santa Sofia and it is the greatest temple of Islam. It is one of Istanbul's most beautiful mosques and the only one to have six minarets making it regal and prestigious. Historians rightly believe that it is a perfect expression of Turkish Islamic art. It is crowded with tourists since the mosque attracts large quantities of visitors; for this reason only small groups are admitted at a time, once they have removed their shoes and covered their heads and shoulders with a brown shawl, provided at the entrance.

The Blue Mosque was built between 1609 and 1616 by Mehmet Ağa, a pupil of the great architect Sinan, and it was commissioned by the young Sultan Ahmet I. You enter the mosque from a large courtyard which has thirty domes supported by twenty-six columns. In the centre there is a beautiful hexagonal *Şardivan* surrounded by six marble columns. At one time this fountain was used for performing ablutions.

You enter the great *Prayer Room* through three large doors, and are immediately taken by surprise by its beauty and dazzled by the light and colour. The Room has a square floor plan and has a central dome twenty-three metres in diameter, supported by four lateral domes which in turn are supported by four great fluted columns.

The proportions of this mosque are striking, making it a masterpiece of elegance and harmony. Light filters into the interior through two hundred and sixty windows and the walls are completely covered by twenty thousand green-blue coloured tiles from Iznik. The name Blue Mosque derives from the colour of the majolica. The carpets are extremely beautiful, some of them are antique, covering the entire floor of the Mosque.

The interior of the richly-decorated Blue Mosque.

THE LARGEST MARKET IN THE WORLD

The Grand Bazaar is in the centre of Istanbul, and is open every day until sunset except Sunday. Once you have entered through one of the large arched gates, you are immersed in a labyrinth of streets, lanes and alleys crammed with an unbelievable array of merchandise of every form, shape and colour in a deafening babble and bustle of tourists, customers and merchants. Here the oriental art of buying and selling is celebrated and its liveliness lasts from dawn to dusk. Visitors are harassed with insistent politeness by a series of "porters" and once caught the customer is shown his merchandise inside and almost always offered

offer. And if you are looking for a pendant without spending a great deal, perhaps finely worked in filigree, or a souvenir, an unusual colourful exotic object, this is the place to go, even if you only want to take away the memory of the occasion.

The Grand Bazaar is almost a millennial structure, dating back to the end of the fifteenth century when Constantinople was conquered by the Turks and it has always been a characteristic element of the spirit and temperament of these people. By the beginning of this century there were four thousand shops, two thousand ateliers as well as five hundred stalls.

Three illustrations of the interior of Istanbul's Grand Bazaar and of the Egyptian Bazaar,
where every kind of merchandise can be found, from carpets, to copper articles and fragrant spices.

a cup of good tea or Turkish coffee. Haggling takes a long time and you bargain sitting down, passing from refusing the initial generally high asking price until the bargain is made at an affordable level. There is an infinite variety of merchandise from articles of great value to colourful knick-knacks.

Antique jewels of great value, an amazing array of carpets of differing quality, leather clothing and leather goods can all be found in the Grand Bazaar. Copper pots, hand-worked sacred images, unusual crystal-ware are all on

Today there are more than four hundred jewellers, goldsmiths, small antique shops, tailors and carpet dealers. This is a place not only for buying or looking, but where you can also enjoy being in one of the five hundred small restaurants and tea and coffee shops to be found in the Grand Bazaar. Those who do not come to see this city within a city, this evocative, noisy labyrinth of smells, sounds and voices, are turning down a unique opportunity and they will be unable to understand the infinite subtlety of the oriental mind.

The Impressive Prayer Room in the Mosque at Eyüp.

The *mihrab* (niche) and the *mimber* (pulpit) are exquisitely carved in white marble. From the *mimber,* in 1826, the Sultan proclaimed the disbandment of the janissaries who had " contributed to the taking of Constantinople." A piece of the black stone of the Kaaba is set in the *mihrab.*

The Mosque of Eyüp

The **Mosque of Eyüp** faces the Golden Horn. It has only two minarets, it is completely white and surrounded by greenery and is a place of faith and pilgrimage for Muslims. It was called Eyüp in memory of Mahomet's disciple Eyüp El Ensari (Job) who was killed in Constantinople bearing the banner of Islam during the

Arab siege which took place between 674 and 678. His remains are buried here.

Eyüp was built in 1458 but following a violent earthquake during which it was completely destroyed, it was rebuilt in the 18th century. To go inside the mosque you pass through two beautiful portals which give on to two courtyards. The first is the larger and paved in marble and the second is planted with ancient trees. The mosque is covered by a central dome and surrounded by eight smaller domes, some larger than others. The *Prayer Room* is light and airy with golden decorations and inscriptions taken from the Koran. The floor carpets, of which one is vast, are woven in bright colours with blue and turquoise highlights. This mosque has a particular tradition becau-

The Monastery of Christ in Chora, now an important Museum.

se it was the place of the Sultans' investiture of rule. The ceremony involved buckling on the sword of Oman. Facing the mosque is an ornate octagonal **mausoleum**, housing the tomb of *Eyüp El Ensari.* The mausoleum is protected by fine and imposing gatework.

The Monastry of Christ in Chora (Kariye Camii)

Close by the sparse remains of Constantine Porphyrogenites's Palace is the **Kariye Camii** (The Rose Mosque), at one time the **Church of Christ in Chora**, which is now a museum. In ancient times it was outside the walls of Constantinople ('in Chora' meant in the country).

This stupendous Byzantine church retains many mosaics made of gold, and its frescoes and decorations are amongst the most precious in Istanbul, perhaps in the world. They were produced during the reign of Andronicus II together with his erudite and favoured counsellor Theodorus Metochite, during the dazzling renaissance in Byzantine art and humanism that took place in Constantinople before its relentless decline began in 1453 following the Turkish occupation. During the Turkish siege, the Byzantines transferred the famous icon of the **Madonna Odigitria** (meaning She Who Points the Way)

The exterior of Süleyman's Mosque.

to the Church of Christ in Chora. The Madonna had once come to Constantinople's assistance, and it was hoped that she might again protect the city.

The Sultan Bayazet II transformed the monastery-church of Christ in Chora into a mosque, but his Grand Vizier, the eunuch Atik Alì Paşha, covered over the mosaics and frescoes with plaster, rather than destroying them. The origins and the story of Christianity are recounted in the mosaics and in the frescoes on the walls. The Church of Christ in Chora had been built by Theodosius II; after the earthquake of 558, the Emperor Justinian ordered its reconstruction, and, during the 12th century, following the wishes of Maria Dukas, (the niece of Isaac Comneno), it was completely restored and embellished. The Church was furnished with an *exonarthex* (exterior vestibule) and a *narthex*, and has a square nave with a semi-circular apse and a dome supported by four columns. On the right hand side of the nave there is the *Parecclesion* (funerary side-chapel) and on the left a two-storeyed corridor.

A tour of the mosaics and wall-frescoes should start with the exonarthex where the frescoes depict *The Infancy of Christ* from his conception. The mosaic depicting the *Massacre of the Innocents* is realistic and disturbing. The decorations on the walls and in the lunettes of the

View of the interior of Süleyman's Mosque.

narthex depict *The Genealogy of Christ* and *The Infancy and Life of the Madonna.* In the central nave there is *The Death of the Madonna* (Dormition) showing her soul represented by the child held in Christ's arms.

In the adjoining chapel there is *The Parecclesion*, an extraordinary fresco of *Last Judgement* and amongst the other stupendous mosaics those depicting *Theodorus Metochite* (his tomb is also noteworthy) *Offering the Church to Christ,* should also be seen.

The Süleymaniye Camii

The Süleymaniye Camii, considered the most beautiful and sumptuous of Istanbul's mosques, reflects the glory and power of the Ottoman Empire and the erudite Sultan, Süleyman known as the Magnificent or Kanuni the Legislator. The mosque was built on a hill-top and dominates the Golden Horn. Sülemaniye was constructed by Sinan the great Ottoman architect, who started work in 1550 and had completed it by 1557. The floor plan of the mosque is almost square with a large decorated dome next to two half-domes supported by columns. Bright light filters through the great dome's thirty-two windows.

The *mihrab* and the *mimber* are worked in pure white inlaid marble with great elegance, as are the windows where the glass is decorated with arabesque floral subjects, and the walls are covered with Iznik tiles with blue, red and turquoise colours on a white background. The praying bench and the shutters are all made of wood inlaid with mother-of-pearl and the floors covered with carpets some of which are of great antiquity.

The mosque, which has four minarets and ten balconies, is

The Hippodrome Square. In the foreground the 15th Century B.C. Egyptian Obelisk.

surrounded by a series of buildings housing the school of medicine, the hospital, the town soup-kitchen, the elementary schools, the *hamam* and the cemetery. It is a small town in itself. Today you can visit the cemetery behind the mosque with the octagonal *Tomb of Süleyman,* covered by a dome and by a columned portico. The interior is richly decorated with blue and white majolica. Above the entrance door a marble tablet with gold numbering records the year of the Sultan Süleyman's death.

The *Tomb of Roxellana,* the Sultan's wife, is much more modest but decorated with refined majolica throughout. Even Sinan, the architect, is buried here in a tomb that he himself designed. In the Sülemaniye Camii, as opposed to the other mosques, the proportions are on an impressive scale, the space is enormous and enveloping. The light that filters through the hundred and thirty-

eight windows is translucent, diaphanous, almost white. There are no shadows, everything must be immediately visible and silence all pervading.

The Hippodrome

The tree-lined square of the Hippodrome is between Santa Sophia and the Blue Mosque. At one time the populace gathered there to watch shows and horse races. It was also the scene of revolts such as the fierce rising against Justinian in 532, and the theatre of political clashes between the Greens and the Blues, members of opposing parties. It was indeed in this square that in 1826 Mahmut II ordered the assassination of the janissaries. The hippodrome was enlarged, modified and developed by Constantine, but its construction dates back to 203 A.D. when it was commissioned by Septimius Severus who wanted a large and imposing building.

It is four hundred metres long and one hundred and twenty metres wide, and had room for around fifty thousand spectators. Of the original hippodrome, nowadays known as **At Meydani** (Horse Square) only three columns remain, the only reminders of its former greatness.

Constantine's Column or the **Walled Obelisk** is thirty-two metres high; according to the inscription (visible at the base of the plinth), it was erected by Constantine Porphyry and later sheathed in bronze gilt.

The **Serpentine Column** is Istanbul's monument of greatest antiquity. It is most unusual, being formed by three intertwining snakes. At one time the snakes' heads supported a golden urn. Originally it was eight metres high, today only five. Its construction was ordered by thirty Greek cities in honour of the god Apollo in 479 A.D. following the Greek victory over the Persians.

The **Egyptian Obelisk**, or **Theodosius's Obelisk** dates from 1490 B.C. and was brought over from Luxor in Egypt to Istanbul; in 390 A.D. Theodosius set it up in the hippodrome. The entire surface of the obelisk is covered with decorations. Scenes of daily life and famous inhabitants of Constantinople are depicted in the bas reliefs. There are spectacular scenes illustrating the Emperor and his children watching the horse-racing.

Dolmabahçe Saray

The Dolmabahçe palace is situated on the European bank of the Bosphorus, on land that has been reclaimed from the sea: the words *Dolma - Bahçe* mean "reclaimed garden". The palace is a typical example of Ottoman architecture, both baroque and sumptuous and its exterior is faced with white marble. The facade faces the sea as does the long gate-work (two hundred and fifty metres) protecting it just above the water-front.

It became, in 1856, after Topkapi, the final residence of the Sultans: it then became the seat of the Turkish Government. The palace is open to the public, on payment, when it is not in use by the Government.

On the ground floor there is a grand reception room with a double staircase: one side gave access to those arriving by sea, the other to those arriving by land. The *ball room* is dramatic and lavish, with a central dome. It was once the throne room with a chandelier equipped with seven hundred and fifty candles. It was a gift from Queen Victoria. In this room Atatürk's coffin is shown to the public: it is also considered to be perhaps the largest ball room in existence. In another room the Sultan Abdül Mecit I's bed can be seen. It is masterpiece of carving and craftsmanship, inlaid with silver and mother-of-pearl.

On the first floor there are rooms and apartments used by the mothers and wives of the Sultans. The *Red Room, the*

Below, the beautiful Dolmabahçe Palace, on the European Bank of the Bosphorus. Facing page, the entrance to the Topkapi Palace.

Porphyry Room, and, above all, the *Panoramic Saloon* where Atatürk took his meals, should be seen. His work was done in the *Azure Room* and in this room he died. In Dolmabahçe Saray there is a tower where the clock always shows 9.05, the time of the death of General Atatürk, the father of the Turkish nation, on November 10th 1938. The palace guide always informs the visitors that the clock will never be altered. Next to the palace, on the sea, you can see the **Dolmabahçe mosque,** built in 1853 , and the Museum of the Turkish Marine, the **Deniz Müzei.**

The Topkapi Saray

The **Topkapi Saray** is behind Santa Sofia on the point of the Seraglio, on one of Istanbul's seven hills between the Golden Horn, the Bosphorus, and the Sea of Marmara. This was the site of Constantine's Imperial Palace. The Topkapi ("Cannon Gate") Palace is now a museum but it was the Sultans' residence for many years. Mahomet II, the Conqueror, began its construction in 1462 and subsequently the Sultans who succeeded him modified it and made additions in accordance with their own taste and style or fantasy, not following any architectural consistency.

The Topkapi Saray is surrounded by high walls and towers and is divided into four courtyards which communicate with one another via imposing portals, which are, however, not opposite each other.

The *Imperial Gate,* in the first courtyard, is the most important: through this gate the Sultan made his entrances and his exits. It was also the lodgings of his private guards, the janissaries. In the buildings nearby were the imperial ovens, the hospital, the powder-magazine and the mint. The latter was used not only to coin money, but also to manufacture gold and silver cutlery for the palace

The Pagoda in the gardens of the Topkapi Palace.
Below, the Throne of Nadir Shah and beneath, a ceremonial throne. Both are in the Topkapi collection.

and to fashion jewellery for the Sultan. On the left of the courtyard the fine sixth century **Church of Saint Irene** can be seen. On the right of the Imperial Gate is the ancient *Executioner's Fountain*, where those condemned to death were executed and their heads put on display.

The **Gate of Well-Being** *(Ortkapo)*, now the tourists' entrance to the museum, has two notable towers with conical roofs. On the left is the **Council Chamber**, the **Kubealti**, looked over by one of the towers. From this room, for four hundred years, the Sultans ruled the Empire. The **Imperial Kitchens** are also worth visiting: they are spacious and well-equipped, furnished with ten conical fireplaces and twenty small domes. Here one thousand one hundred cooks prepared meals for the inhabitants of Topkapi who numbered five thousand. Next door is a spectacular room where the third most important collection of Chinese porcelain, after Beyjing and Dresden, is displayed. There is also a notable **Silver Collection**, made up of three thousand objects, on display. The rarest piece is an antique vase that once belonged to Süleyman the Magnificent.

The **Gate of Happiness** leading onto the third courtyard *(Endurum)* was also called the Gate of the White Eunuchs. Here were the dormitories of the more important eunuchs. Ahead is the **Audience Chamber**, entirely covered in majolica, and twenty columns support the roof. Under this portico was placed the famous *Throne of Ishmail*, set with pearls, rubies and gold that the Sultan had plundered from the King of Persia.

Here ambassadors and great dignitaries were received and entertained with banquets and ceremonies. The room houses a splendid *collection of garments*, made of silk, velvet and brocade belonging to various sultans and made by the imperial tailors of Bursa. The *Treasury* is also located in the third courtyard. The most important piece is the *Spoon Merchant's Diamond,* the *Kasikçi Elmasi.* It is a stupendous gem fashioned in the form of a spear weighing eighty-six carats framed by forty-nine diamonds. It appears to have been bought from a workman who exchanged it for three miserable spoons. Other pieces of great value include the *Festal Throne,* entirely covered in gold weighing two hundred and fifty kilograms, and the famous *dagger*, Topkapi's symbol, which has three enormous emeralds on the sides and the fourth on the hilt where there is also a hidden time-piece.

The final part of the visit should be reserved for the **Harem**, the **House of Felicity**, of which only certain rooms are open to the public accompanied by authorised guides. The Harem is divided into three courtyards: the first of the Sultan Valid, the second for the domestic servants and the third for the favourites and for the wives who had had children. The **Sovereign's Room** is the largest in the Harem and is furnished with Chinese vases, ceramics, precious crystals and large Murano mirrors which conceal secret doors. The triumph of sophistication in the Harem is the **Fountain Room**, or **Murat III's Room**, where water flows unceasingly, the walls are all decorated with majolica and panels surrounding the bronze fireplace depict flowering plum-trees.

THE HAREM: "HOUSE OF HAPPINESS"

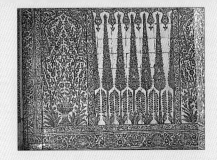

The West has always been fascinated by the notion of the harem conjuring up fantasies of a place of sensuality and forbidden desires. Paintings and literature have handed down images of beautiful junoesque women whose only task was to satisfy every desire of the lord, the sultan. Historically the harem was also a place of royal instruction ruled by strict discipline with a rod of iron. The word harem derives from harim which denotes a place reserved for women and children.

Before Islamic religion, harems existed in Assyrian-Babylonian and Egyptian palaces. The women who lived in the harem were almost always foreigners or slaves, or young children sold by their parents. The women most in demand were Circassian as they were thought to be the most beautiful and intelligent, like the slave Roxellana who became the wife of the powerful sultan Süleyman the Magnificent, a lover and patron of the arts.

Once they had entered the harem,

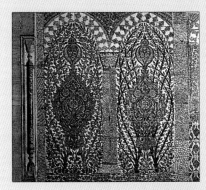

Three illustrations of the harem showing the elegance and the luxury of the interior.

the odalisques were educated and taught the arts and practices of seduction but they were also given the elements of general culture. Once they had passed a final exam, the odalisques were assigned a task

or role within the harem but they were never allowed to leave the harem. Many odalisques died or were pensioned off in the Old Seraglio (Palace of Tears) without ever having seen their master. It was the task of the Chief eunuch to choose which concubine would spend the night in the sultan's bed. The eunuchs were dark-skinned and castrated at birth, but they enjoyed considerable privileges .

The only people to have access to the harem other than the eunuchs were the Muezzin who were blind from birth. The most powerful woman, even in the harem, was

the Sultan Valid, or the sultan's mother, who with the assistance of the eunuchs, administered the funds and the palace expenses. She would give orders to the Grand Vizier and would provide them

and other functionaries working for the Empire with brides selected from her odalisques.

In the Topkapi palace the harem consisted of four hundred rooms arranged around courtyards and corridors. The sultan's mother occupied forty of them for herself and her court.

Although the harem was like a fortress, it had every kind of convenience and was home to between three and six hundred people. In the harem's hierarchy wives with children ranked next after the sultan's mother, then wives without children, then the favourites and

finally the novices.

Intrigues, rivalry and jealousy were rife and often the women in the harem would use their powers to determine the future of the Ottoman Empire.

The Selimiye Camii at Edirne

EDIRNE

Edirne, the ancient Hadrianopolis (Adrianople), and the capital of Thrace (bordering on Greece and Bulgaria) was founded in 125 A.D. by the Roman Emperor, Hadrian. It had an important role as the gateway from Europe to the East. It was from here that Constantine set out to defeat Licinius and Frederick the Great known as Barbarossa stopped here with the Third Crusade. In 1363, for a century, Edirne became the capital of the Ottoman Empire. After the First World War and the collapse of the Ottoman Empire General Atatürk was able to give the town back to Turkey detaching it from Greek rule. Today Edirne is a city of 120,000 inhabitants but visitors to Turkey should not pass by without seeing the splendid mosques and the old part of the city which has retained its oriental character.

The *Three-Galleried Mosque*, **Üç Şerefeli Camii**, was built between 1438 and 1447 and is an example of Selçuk Turkish architecture. Its interior courtyard which has a central fountain for ablutions; its distinctive feature is one of its four minarets which has three balconies. The minarets were erected over differing periods.

The **Selimiye Camii** on the hill looks over the whole city of Edirne. It was built on the orders of Selim II between 1556 and 1574 by the famous Janissary architect, Sinan.

The Interior of the Selimiye Camii.

The interior is particularly evocative since it has an octagonal structure, and the dome has a diameter of thirty-two metres. The mosque has nine hundred and ninety-nine windows, and the pulpit (*mimber*), where the Iman preaches on Fridays) is made of carved marble and the niche (*mihrab*, facing towards Mecca) is covered in coloured tiles from Iznik. Today in the mosque's old Theology School (*madrasa*) there is an interesting **Ethnographic and Archaeological Museum**.

In 1436 the **Muradye Camii**, the mosque commissioned by the Sultan Murat in the form of a T, was completed. It is typically Ottoman and was part of the *Convent of the Mevlevi* (dancing dervishes) as is demonstrated by the sur-

viving stone tombs. The **Eski Camii** or "Old Mosque" dates from the fifteenth century. Its structure is rectangular and there are nine domes, whose supporting columns on the front facade are Roman, as can be clearly seen, and were probably removed from an ancient palace. Facing the mosque is the **Bedesten**, the well-known market bazaar covered by numerous domes and behind, a large **Caravanserai**, built by Sinan for the Grand Vizier Rüsten Pasa. Every year at Edirne, in May and June, in the ruins of the ancient *Sarayici Ottoman Palace*, the annual championship of *Turkish Wrestling* takes place. This national sport is immensely popular, rather like the Italian passion for football, and is accompanied by music and prayers.

WRESTLING, TURKEY'S NATIONAL SPORT

Wrestling, the national game in Turkey is a body to body contest between two unarmed contestants. It is an ancient, popular sport with a long tradition that goes back perhaps as far as the Etruscans, Egyptians and the Greeks. All over Turkey the fighting spirit is widely felt, especially in the summer when contests between athletes take place, but

ce that includes politicians, even foreign ones. Here, the champion of the year is declared. Kirkpinar literally means "forty cascades". There is a legend, told endlessly by the Turks, that two contestants fought day and night for an endless time until the public found them dead, but still standing, with their arms twisted as if they were still fighting.

At the site suddenly forty streams began to spurt forth water.

An the Kirkpinar tournament forty athletes, called the Pehlivan, grease their bodies with a mixture of olive oil and water, they then parade before the public before splitting up into couples and starting the contest. To make the contest as fair as possible a man rather like a referee, dressed in eccentric clothes, watches over and controls the game, but without the power of stopping it, except in cases were a move is thought to be dangerous or illegal. It is a contest by elimination and the last remaining athlete is declared champion of the year.

Most bouts last about an hour, but when the contestants are evenly matched they can go on for much longer.

The supporters of the ancient sport regret escalating violence amongst the public, especially when one of the favourites loses. Turkish wrestling is immensely popular with men and boys, mostly from the country, who come in search of fame and fortune.

The Monument to the Wrestlers in the centre of Edirne. Above, Turkish Wrestlers at the beginning of a Tournament.

there are also fights between bulls, camels and dogs. The public place bets, shout and scream exactly like football supporters. The most important tournament takes place in July at Kirkpinar, near Edirne, in front of an audien-

A view of the exterior of the Green Mosque.

IZNIK (NICEA)

Iznik is famous throughout the world for its green-blue tiles (once again in fashion) which are found in the finest mosques. Iznik was formerly called Nicea, after the wife of Lysimachus, one of Alexander the Great's generals, who conquered the city in the fourth century B.C. Under the protection of Rome (Pliny the Younger was one of its governors) city walls, temples and theatres were built.

Two important ecumenical councils of the Christian Church took place here (in 325 the Arian heresy was condemned, and in 787 the Empress Irene sided against the Iconoclasts). After the first and the fourth crusade Nicea was conquered after a year's fighting by the Ottomans and the Sultan Orhar renamed it Iznik. Since then the city has been embellished with monuments and became the most important centre for the production of glazed tiles.

Selim I, nicknamed the Merciless, conquered the city of Tabriz in Persia and deported its tilemakers to Iznik.

Only the four city gates survive from the Roman period. The first, the *Lefke Kapsis*, built in honour of the Emperor Hadrian in 123 A.D., is constructed from three consecutive gates.

Only a few stones and ruins remain of the second gate, the *Gate of Lake, Göl Kapisi* in Turkish, and little survives of **Constantine's Palace**. Of the other two, the *Istanbul Kapisi* and the Yenişchir Kapisi, the former is without doubt the finer and in a better state of preservation.

The **Church of Divine Wisdom**, or **Haghia Sophia**, nowadays a mosque, is in the town centre and in it there is a fresco depicting Jesus, Mary and John the Baptist and a fine mosaic floor. Near the Lefke Gate if the **Yeşil Camii**, the Green Mosque with a single minaret. Its tiles are indeed glazed green. The **Haci Özbek** mosque, built in 1332, is thought by historians to be first mosque of the Ottoman age.

A Panorama of the city. Facing page, sporting facilities for Skiing on Mount Olympus, near Bursa.

BURSA

Bursa is a typically Turkish city, rich in gardens and fruit trees; a city of cotton and silk, and of the Turkish shadow theatre, a theatrical form encouraged by the Sultan Selim I. It is also the city of the *kebab*, the national meat dish made from lamb or mutton, cut into thin strips and served on top of a kind of pitta bread (*pide*), and moistened with melted butter, tomato sauce and yoghurt. Bursa, an asiatic city of a million inhabitants, rises on the foothills of Mount Uludağ, called in the past Mount Olympus of Mysia, where there is a large national park and a centre for winter sports.

Bursa, known as Prusa by the Byzantines, was occupied by the Romans. Thanks to the Apostle Andrew, it became an important city for Christianity. Justinian, in the first instance, encouraged the growth of the silk industry, and built a palace there as well as the **Eski Kaplica Baths**, which were later adapted by the Ottomans to become, perhaps, the finest in Turkey. Today they are in perfect working order and open to men and women. At one time Queen Theodora, Justinian's wife, took the waters here.

Bursa was later taken by the Selçuks and then retaken by the Byzantines, but in 1326, under the Ottomans, it became the Empire's capital, and acquired its present name. In 1363, as we have already mentioned, Edirne became the capital. There are one hundred and twenty five mosques in Bursa: the largest is the **Ulu Camii**, rectangular in shape, and built between 1413 and 1421 for Beyazit I. It has twenty domes supported by twelve columns. Inside there

The exterior of the Great Mosque or Ulu Camii.

is a prayer room, a marble basin with a fountain with three steps for ablutions; the pulpit is made of cedar wood. There are attractive inscriptions from the Koran on the walls, executed in perfect Arabic script. Facing one another, the **Yeşil Camii** (*Green Mosque*) and the **Yeşil Türbe** (*Green Mausoleum*) were both commissioned by the Sultan Çelebi I, whose remains are buried here in the octagonal tomb, covered in green majolica. The mosque was constructed beneath the Sultan's apartments, and its facade is inlaid with white marble. The *mihrab* (the niche facing Mecca) is fifteen metres high and is entirely covered in majolica, as is the interior of the mosque, a triumph of colour and harmony (hence the name Green Mosque).

The **Beyazit Camii**, built in 1391, should not be missed, nor should other buildings such as the school, the kitchens for the poor and the hospital nor the **Muradiye Camii** Mosque, near the citadel, built in the fifteenth century in the form of a "T". The glazed majolica inside is azure-coloured, but the tiles covering the *mihrab* are white and

blue. There are twelve tombs from various periods in the mosque's garden, some of which are elaborately decorated, and others more simple; amongst these is the unusual tomb of the Sultan Murat II, which has an aperture high up in the dome allowing rain water to filter through (the Sultan believed in the mystic purifying powers of water).

Before leaving Bursa visit the **Bedesten**, a covered bazaar built at the end of the fourteenth century, destroyed in an earthquake and later reconstructed. There you can buy not only the amusing and famous puppets from Karagöz (they have black eyes) made of coloured camel skin, but also fine silks, damasked velvet, and brightly-coloured organza taken from the original designs.

All the Sultans' clothes made of silk and brocade (now on display in the Topkapi Palace) were made by the imperial tailors at Bursa and even today, using the city's silk, some of the finest silk Turkish carpets are made here. They are woven with flower motifs, tulips and roses, and have more than a million stitches per square metre.

TROY

Close by the Dardanelle Straights, Hellespont in ancient times, lies the legendary city of **Troy**. It is essential to go there because it is a mythical place in the history of the West, where Homer sings of its mythical heroes in the *Odyssey* and the *Iliad* and the beginnings of Western literature. There is not a great deal left to see in Troy today, but its ruins speak to us in a way that time has been unable to destroy. There are traces of succeeding civilisations in Troy's many layers of earth, civilisations that replaced one another dating back as far as 4,000 B.C. Archaeological excavations began in Troy in 1871 on the hill of Hisarlik, directed by a German named Heinrich Schliemann who was stubborn, far-sighted and rich, and they still continue today. The various levels that can be seen are numbered from I to IX and each one can be followed by observing the instructions on precise indicator boards.

At **Troy I** there are the remains of two towers that supported a gate. **Troy II** is reached by a stone-slabbed ramp enclosing, according to Schliemann, the ancient treasury of Priam, King of the Trojans. **At Troy III and IV** (2,500-2,000 B.C.) there are the remains of a few roads and houses that may have formed a village. Troy V preserves the ruins of buildings surrounded by a wall. **Troy VI** displays an open space two hundred metres in diameter with remains of thick walls ninety metres long and six metres high, protecting a citadel that had trade links with Mycenae and Greece. This, according to the Homeric tradition, was the birth place of Priam. **Troy VII** dates from the time of the heroes narrated by Homer and was, according to the archaeologists, burned by the Greeks around 1,200 B.C. Troy VII was rebuilt by a population that originated in the Balkans and then, for the next four hundred years, fell into oblivion.

From the terrace on the **Acropolis** of Troy the entire panorama of the ruins can be seen with the sea in the distance. Troy VIII dates from 700 B.C. when the town

Detail of the excavations at the Ancient City of Troy.

was reconstructed by Greek colonists and the temple of Athena dated from this period. Later the town was sacked by the Persians and became under General Lysimachus "New Ilium". The ruins of the **Gate of Dardanus**, where, in the *Iliad*, the Trojan hero Hector was killed by Achilles, are most evocative. By 85 B.C., during the times of Julius Caesar, Ilium Novum, or Troy IX had become rich and prosperous. Here Augustus and Caracalla, the Roman Emperors, spent long periods of time. It was also the see of a Bishopric, but after its conquest by the Turks, Troy once again fell into oblivion.

There is an unusual attraction for current visitors: next to the museum before the entrance to the archaeological area, there is a large reconstruction of the *wooden horse*. Tourists are allowed inside, it affords a marvellous view of the city. It is of course the famous **Trojan Horse**, the instrument of antique deception, placed here to record the Trojans' defeat at the hands of the Achaeans.

Left, the reconstruction of Troy's legendary wooden horse. Below, a view of the city's theatre.

The remains of Greek ruins in the Temple of Athena.

ASSOS

Assos, or rather the ruins of ancient Assos, is located high up on the promontory of the Gulf of Edremit, facing the island of Lesbos on the Aegean Sea, where the poet Sappho was born.

Assos, or **Behramke**, is now a village which lives off agriculture, sheep-rearing and embroidery but in the summer it is invaded by numerous tourists (there are private beaches). The city's origins date back to 500 B.C., when the Greeks established a colony here. It was later conquered by the Lydians before falling into the hands of the Persians. During the fourth century B.C. Aristotle was invited by the Governor of Assos, the eunuch Herias, to move there. He accepted, married, and tried, with the help of philosophers, mathematicians and scientists, to establish Plato's Republic, the ideal city state there.

In 1330 Assos became an Ottoman city. The *Ottoman Bridge* at the village entrance dates from this period, but only the ruins of the Temple of Athena, built around 530 B.C. with low columns and simple modest capitals survive from the Greek remains. Higher up on the hill is the **Murad Hüdavendigar Camii**, the oldest Anatolian mosque, built in 1359 with a large dome, perhaps on the foundations of an early Christian Church: in fact a few crosses are visible by the entrance.

The magnificent ruins of Temple of Trajan. Opposite, the Way of the Acropolis.

BERGAMA -PERGAMUM

Six kilometres currently separate modern Bergama on the plain from the ancient city of Pergamum on the hill. Bergama is a small, lively agricultural town with fifty thousand inhabitants, surrounded by orchards, olive groves and vineyards. It is very pleasant to stop by the roadside, to make way for the flocks of sheep and goats going out to pasture, to see the brightly-painted lorries transporting their produce and to meet cheerful women with covered heads astride overladen mules.

In the town centre there is a noisy bazaar market where all kinds of things are bought and sold, from old household objects, to shoes, copper, polished carvings, old and new. And then, of course, the famous Bergama carpets, rigorously made of wool with geometrical designs and almost always coloured red. It is not hard to meet women sitting in front of their houses who like to invite tourists into their homes to show them their looms, and possibly sell them a carpet. Towards the end of May the town has a Gastronomic Festival with folklore and crafts and fills up with visitors. There is a mythological story which tells how Andromache, after Achilles had killed Hector, became the slave of Neptolemus (Achilles' Son) by whom she had three children. One of these, Pergamum, was the founder of the city. But, leaving mythology aside, Pergamum did indeed have a glorious past. Lysimachus, Alexander the Great's gifted general, enlarged its boundaries, and then, during the reign of Eumenes II (197-159 B.C.) it grew both culturally and commercially. Eumenes II was a writer, scientist and patron of the arts and he especially loved Hellenistic culture, which he endlessly tried to preserve. He enriched Pergamum with monuments, buildings and pieces of sculpture. The famous library which rivalled the library of Alexandria in Egypt, was established at this time; and under his rule parchment, writing paper made from camel or goat skin, began to be used so as to punish the pharaoh who had jealously refused the sell Egyptian papyrus. Schools of medicine, philosophy, astronomy and mathematics were all established at this time, as

were textile, leather and engineering schools. In 130 B.C. the kingdom of Pergamum was inherited by the Romans, bequeathed by Attalus III. The population duly increased and new monuments embellished the city. Pergamum's decline began with the Byzantines as it was continually subject to Arab invasions. It became an Ottoman city in the fourteenth century. Then again the city grew larger.

Today's visit should commence either with the **Acropolis**, or with **Pergamum's** celebrated **library**, second only to the Egyptian library at Alexandria. The foundations of five rooms are discernible. During excavations a large statue of Athena was found inside, but the library had other sculptures portraying Homer, Sappho and Hirodicus, the inventor of parchment. Anthony, through love, presented the whole library to his wife, Cleopatra.

Nearby are the ruins of what was once Eumenes II's royal palace, built in 200 B.C. and an imposing temple, currently undergoing restoration, dedicated to the Emperor Trajan after he had become a deity. **Trajan's Temple** was built on a terraced outcrop dominating the plain below. It was once surrounded by white marble Corinthian columns, some of which have been re-erected on their pediments. Using the foundations of the **Doric Temple of Athena**, which originally had sixty-six columns, the Byzantine Emperor Justinian constructed a church in the sixth century A.D.

The **theatre** is certainly the most original monument, constructed on the form of an open fan rather than the traditional semi-circular model. It was built by the Hellenes around the third century B.C. on a steep hill and was sub-

Two splendid views of the Temple of Trajan.

sequently altered by the Romans. Then the theatre held ten thousand spectators seated on eighty rows of steps, and still, despite the passing of time, it has wonderful acoustics. Only the base remains of **Pergamum's great altar dedicated to Zeus**, the altar itself and the relief depicting the Battle of the Giants are now in the Pergamum Museum in Berlin. Three large trees shade what was once one of the master-pieces of architecture, frieze and Greek sculpture: the altar was erected during Eumenes II's golden age, as a thanksgiving to the Gods Zeus and Athena after the King's victory over the Galatians in 190 B.C.

The oldest monument in Pergamum, dating from the third century B.C. is the **Temple of Demeter**. It is in the Ionian style and could hold eight hundred spectators during festivals or rites in honour of the goddess Demeter and her daughter Persephone. Two columns of the propylaea and the great altar are still standing. On the opposite side of the temple is the Gymnasium, a vast structure divided into three sectors: an upper, central and lower section. The upper Gymnasium, the largest of the three, was reserved for adults, the central for ephebes, adolescents aged from fifteen to eighteen, and the lower section for children. Some parts, such as the *lavatorium*, the *frigidarium* and the *tepidarium* have withstood the ravages of time, although vegetation tends to cover over the area.

The colonnaded **Via Sacra**, or the **Via Tecta**, as it was renamed by the Romans who restored it, leads to the Asclepeium, Pergamum's most important monument. It was the sacrarium to vitality and medicine. The temple was in fact dedicated to Asclepius, the god of healing, whose

The "Red Hall" dedicated to the cult of Serapis. Facing page, the remains of the Roman Theatre.

cult animals were snakes, symbols of the life force. The two famous doctors, Satyros and Galen, who created modern medicine, studied and taught here in the second century A.D. The **Asclepeium** reached the height of its fame under the Romans and many emperors came to the temple to be cured. It had been constructed by a beneficent citizen of Pergamum called Archia who had recovered from a serious illness. In modern Bergama there are two interesting museums: the **Ethnographical Museum** and the **Archaeological Museum**. In the Ethnographical Museum, as well as a valuable Commentary on Medicine, there is a collection of antique carpets from Pergamum.

The Archaeological Museum displays objects found in the excavations, Greek and Roman statues including a nude statue of the Emperor Hadrian and a statue of the Goddess of Victory bearing a cornucopia. There are further statues in terracotta and marble such as the charming first century A.D. head of Eros and other friezes and funerary steles. The last part of the visit should be reserved for the **Kizil Avlu** or Red Hall, dedicated to the cult of Serapis and the Egyptian gods. It is called the red hall on account of its construction in red bricks and it was transformed by the Byzantines into a basilica dedicated to St. John. The Ottomans later turned it into a mosque.

IZMIR (SMYRNA)

According to legend, Homer, the father of all poets, was born in **Izmir** the modern name for Smyrna. The city lies on the foothills of *Kadifekale* (ancient Mount Pagus) in a beautiful bay in the Gulf of Izmir. It is Turkey's third largest city in terms of population and is second only to Istanbul in terms of industry and commercial activity. It is a modern, very western city with wide streets and palm-lined avenues along the sea and imposing glass-fronted buildings built after the fire in 1922 which razed it to the ground. Smyrna is constructed on undulating hills where tobacco and cotton are worked, the Muscat grape is cultivated to produce excellent wine and where the fruit, which grows abundantly, is dried and exported.

One district of modern Smyrna, now called Bayrakli, was

View of the City with the coast.

already inhabited by the Hittites 2,000 years before the birth of Christ. Eolian colonists, followed by Ionians in the eleventh century B.C., successively conquered the city and in 600 B.C. it was utterly destroyed by Aliatte, King of the Lydians but it was rebuilt by Alexander the Great and Lysimachus. In 27 A.D. the Romans annexed Smyrna to the Empire and embellished the city with new roads and monuments and it developed into a cultural centre. It was again destroyed in the earthquake of 178 A.D. and reconstructed by Marcus Aurelius. Under the Emperor Constantine Smyrna became an important Bishopric. It was later sacked by the Arabs, before falling first to the Selçuk Turks, followed by the Genoese, the Crusaders and the Venetians, before becoming part of the Ottoman Empire under the Sultan Mehmet I Çelebi, in 1415. After the First World War Smyrna, which had passed to Greece

TURKEY, THE CRADLE OF THE CLASSICAL WORLD

Whoever comes as a visitor to Turkey today will be struck by its natural beauty and fascinated by the ruins of ancient temples, roads, and cities. But they will be unable to prevent themselves from continually perceiving, in a subtle way, the magnetism of an immense culture that had its cradle here, even though its later glory took place in Greece.

In these lands of Asia Minor and in its larger cities that once prospered and flourished, lived and worked the greatest minds in classical

pid sky that antiquity's greatest philosopher, Aristotle, collected his famous library and elaborated a vision of the world, both physical and ethical, that would dominate Western culture well beyond medieval times.

For at least seven centuries this country gave rise to so many names who populate the philosophical and poetical Olympus that to give a complete list would be redundant, if not impossible. From the great rector of Teos, Elios Aristides, the philosopher from Smyrna, to

"The Three Philosophers" by Giorgione. The Painting hangs in the Kunsthistorische Museum in Vienna. Left, bronze bust of Homer.

antiquity. Homer, the great poet who created the epic, was born here; it is not certain whether he was from Smyrna or Chio. Ephesus, the illustrious and erudite Ephesus, was home to Heracleitus and Democritus, the fathers of philosophy. The founder of historical science, Herodotus, wrote at Halicarnassus. The delicate love poetry of Anacreon (the lyricist of wine and intoxication) springs from this sea.

Pliny the Elder, the great naturalist who died at Pompei after the eruption of Vesuvius, and his nephew, Pliny the Younger, were both governors of Bitinia. And it was under this lim-

that happy couple of decisive thinkers from Miletus, Anaximenes and Anaximander.

From the great scientist Taletus to Hecataeus, considered to be the father of ancient geography to Apollonius, the illustrious mathematician from Perge. Tramping through barren Turkish countryside and watching its translucent seas and craggy mountains, if the visitor listens carefully, he can hear the murmur of those far off times from the very landscape and from the ancient ruins, the murmur of the time when that immense culture, of which we are all children and heirs, was born.

The celebrated "Way of the Palms" at Izmir.

under the terms of the Treaty of Sèvres, was reconquered by the Turks, led by General Mustafa Kemal Atatürk.
From the **Kadifekale** citadel (*Velvet Fortress*) the whole city can be seen, including the sparse remains of the **Agora**, built by Alexander the Great and it was reconstructed by Marcus Aurelius after the earthquake of 178 A.D. There are now only a few *Corinthian columns* left in the Agora and some mutilated *Roman Statues* of Poseidon, Demeter and Artemis. The crowded and well-stocked **Small Bazaar,** close by the Agora, sells dried fruit,

spices and flowers, and there are amusing workshops where Turkey's famous narghile is crafted. Not far off is the **Konak Meydani**, the square with the modern *Clock-Tower*, built in the moorish style, and the sixteenth-century **Hisar Camii**. The **Archaeological Museum** and the **Ethnographical Museum** are both interesting and should not be missed. The former is located in the *Kültur Parki*, and houses a collection of objects discovered during excavations and a fine collection of Roman sculpture. The latter displays ancient Turkish art and crafts.

EPHESUS

Numerous remains and disinterred monuments give archaeologists reason to believe that Ephesus was inhabited as early as the fourteenth century B.C. Strabo, the Greek historian, asserted that the city had been founded by the Amazons and that its population, partly Carians and partly Lydians, worshipped the Great Goddess Artemis to whom they dedicated an impressive temple, the *Artemision*, of which only a few columns survive. In 334 B.C. Ephesus was conquered by Alexander the Great who initiated the reconstruction of the temple which had been set on fire by Hierostatus on the very night that the Macedonian champion was born. Ephesus became a great capital of Asia Minor after 133 B.C. when it became subject to Rome, and it also evolved as a centre for commerce. Amongst all the Roman-dominated cities in Anatolia, Ephesus certainly has the best preserved and appreciated monuments but above all it is the city where the quality of Roman life can still be breathed today, and where one can form an impression of what life was like at that time. Goths from Crimea conquered the city and looted the Temple of Artemis, then considered to be one of the wonders of the ancient world, and the city's decline dates from then. It was from here that first Paul the Apostle and then John began to spread Christianity. St Paul, who came from Tarsus, spent three years at Ephesus and founded the first of the seven churches mentioned in the Book of Revelations, before being ousted by Ephesian silversmiths. St. John lived here with the Virgin Mary while he wrote his gospel. In 100 A.D. St John was buried in the city and Justinian erected a basilica over his tomb.

The Street of Curetes, Ephesus's main street which connected the Library to the Agora.
Left, the remains of the beautiful Library of Celsus.

In 431 A.D. Theodosius II convened the Third Council at Ephesus, during which the Nestorian heresy was condemned and the Virgin Mary's divine maternity affirmed. The **Library of Celsus**, reconstructed by Austrian archaeologists, is without doubt one of Ephesus' more important monuments. It was erected by Tiberius Julius Aquila in memory of his father, Julius Celsus Polimeanus (pro-consul in Asia) in 135 A.D. His *sarcophagus*, of fine carved marble, is situated in the funerary chamber underneath the library. The two-storied building has a sumptuously decorated facade with Corinthian columns and capitals together with niches filled with statues representing Wisdom and Intelligence. Three doors lead into the great *reading room*, which in antiquity had a wooden roof, and where, in the centre, there stood a statue of Athena. The marble-lined aligned walls contained niches

where the parchment scrolls were kept. At that time the library's collection amounted to around twelve thousand scrolls. Hollow spaces were constructed behind the walls (a great engineering feat) preventing damp from damaging the scrolls. The main road, the street of the **Curetes**, runs through the centre between the Library of Celsus and the Agora. Numerous buildings gave onto this street which was paved in marble and stone. On each side there was a colonnaded portico behind which galleries paved with mosaics provided access to private dwellings, shops and workshops. Some of the inscriptions on the columns are clearly visible, adjacent to statues of citizens who contributed towards the birth of the city. The street was reconstructed after its destruction by an earthquake during the fourth century A.D. It was called the street of the Curetes in memory of a community of priests called the Curetes who worshipped Artemis who every year organised dramatic displays in honour of the goddess at Ortigia, near Ephesus. The **Odeum**, or "**Small Theatre**" on the slopes of Mount Panayir next to the *Prytaneion*, now the town hall, is in a good state of preservation. It was built in 150 A.D. by a rich Ephesian named Publius Vedius Antoninus. It is semi-circular and originally it was certainly roofed over. Its capacity was around 1,500 people. Like most theatres of antiquity it had a *cavea*, stage and orchestra. The *podium* was made of marble as were the spectators' benches. The audience entered through two paradoi, one at either side, or by stairs leading to the paradoi. The Odeum was not only used for dramatic performances and musical concerts but it was also the meeting place (*buleuterio*) for city representatives from the *Bule*. The ruins that can be seen by the eastern side of the theatre are the Baths of Varius, probably privately owned, dating from the second century A.D.

The **Large Theatre** is Ephesus' most picturesque monument, its elevated position dominates the entire valley and it could seat over 20.000 people on sixty-six rows of steps. It was built by the Romans in the first century A.D. on the remains of a Greek theatre during the reign of Claudius and it was modified under Nero. Like all theatres it had a *cavea* (one hundred and fifty four metres in diameter), orchestra (thirty-four metres in diameter), and stage (eighteen metres high). If the *Buletos* met in the Odeum, this was the meeting place for the *Demos*, the peoples' assembly of male citizens.

It was in this great theatre that Ephesian silversmiths who worshipped the Goddess Artemis revolted against St Paul and his followers, forcing them to leave Ephesus. The theatre's facade was ornate: there were three rows of columns with niches and statues and the galleried entrances to the theatre are still visible today.

Not far from the Odeon are the remains of the **monument to Memmius,** commissioned by Augustus in the I century B.C. to honour Cornelius Silla's grandchild.

Hadrian's Temple, in the Corinthian style, was built along the Street of the Curetes in 138 A.D. and was restored by Austrian archaeologists. It is one of Ephesus' most attractive and elegant monuments. The four Corinthian columns in the centre support a finely decorated pediment in the centre of which is an elegant female bust: Tyche, the god-

Below, the spectacular Theatre at Ephesus, which could seat 20,000 spectators. Opposite, the remains of Memmius' monument, I century B.C.

dess who was the guardian of the city. Above the temple door leading to the cella there is a highly decorated tympanum with a sculpture representing Medusa. On the facade, in front of the columns, four statue bases have survived with the inscriptions of the names of four emperors: Diocletian, Maximian, Galerius and Constantius Chlorus. In the cella there is a plinth that at one time supported a statue of Hadrian. On an architrave there is an inscription that the temple was dedicated to the Emperor "Divo Adriano" by P. Quintilius.

The **Dwellings on the Slope**, also called the **Slope Palaces**, were luxurious houses of the rich. They were built on the slopes of Mount Phion and they have an unusual structure as the roof of each house forms the terrace of the next. Almost all of them had three storeys and they were constructed around a peristyle (a courtyard with a columned portico), with a central fountain. The floors were paved with mosaics and almost all the walls frescoed with scenes from mythology. Two of these can be seen, one next to the other, which have been completely restored. The first house dates from the first century A.D. as does the second which has two peristyles and which was restored and modified up to the seventh century. Continuing along the street of the Curetes, behind

the *Baths of Scholasticia*, there is a further house with an atrium, which was a *Brothel*. Nothing remains of the first floor, but on the ground floor some of the walls have retained their frescoes. The mosaic on the floor of the dining room represents the four seasons. The baths were equipped with hot water and at the back there is a pool with mosaics featuring a woman, a mouse and a slave. During restoration work a terracotta statue of Priapus with an enormous phallus was found and it can now be seen in Ephesus' museum.

A few Ionian columns and a perfectly restored wall survive from the **Church of the Virgin Mary**. This is an important church for Christians because it was the first church to be dedicated to the Virgin Mary. The Ecumenical Council convened by Theodosius II proclaiming the Immaculate Conception of the Virgin Mary in 431 A.D. was also held in this basilica. The Church of the Virgin or the Basilica of the Council was erected in the fourth century using the foundations of a second century B.C. basilica structure called the *Museion*. Three naves with columns and balustas were added together with a circular baptistery with a central font. Some of the floor slabs bear inscriptions and others are decorated. The marble *omphalon*, in the centre of the Church, was brought from the Baths of the Port.

Left, the remains of the Temple of Hadrian with the mosaic way in the foreground.
Below, an interior of one of the private houses known as the "Slope Palaces".

Above, the House of the Virgin.
Opposite, above, a view of the Fortress of Selçuk; below, the remains of the Church of St. John.

The **House of the Virgin** is a church on the plan of a cross surmounted by a dome. It is almost entirely reconstructed. It is immersed in the silent green countryside at Panaya Kapulu, a small locality not far from the ruins of Ephesus. In the apse there is a statue of the Virgin (placed there a hundred years ago) and a simple altar. There was once a kitchen in the small central area which is paved in grey marble. Excavations brought to light pieces of charcoal and traces of wood. In the back room, to the south of the altar, there was a bedroom. There is a fountain near the house, the *Fountain of the Virgin*, and its water is said to have miraculous powers. The house is a place of pilgrimage for Christians, Orthodox and Catholic, and Muslims (Meryemana is recognised as a saint by Islam). Every year, on August 15th, believers of all three faiths gather here to celebrate the Assumption of the Virgin. Many ex-votos adorn the House of the Virgin which has been visited by three Popes: John XXIII, Paul VI and John Paul II. Traditionally, the Virgin Mary was thought to have lived in Ephesus for many years with St. John (from 37 to 48 A.D.) after the death of Jesus Christ. Some claim that she was even buried here at the age of sixty-three, though Christians maintain that she was buried in Jerusalem, on Mount Sion, where there is now the Church of Dormition. Before reaching the **Selçukk Fortress**, you come to the **Church of St. John**, thought to be the most important Byzantine building un Ephesus. It was built by Justinian and Queen Theodora during the sixth century A.D. on the ruins of a small church erected over the *Tomb of St. John* who died at Ephesus in 100 A.D. At a later stage thick walls were built around the basilica with twenty towers and three gates to defend it from Arab attacks. When Ephesus was conquered by the Selçuks in 1330 it was first transformed into a mosque and then into a bazaar. Excavations of the basilica began in 1926 and are still being undertaken. The entrance is through the **Gate of Persecution**, surmounted by two imposing towers, which leads into a courtyard and then into the remains of the church. The church was forty metres wide and one hundred and ten metres long, and constructed on the pattern of the cross. There are three naves covered by domes supported by brick and marble pilasters. The Saint's tomb is above the crypt facing the apse. The *Baptistery* was octagonal and faced with marble, and the font was embellished with arches and columns.

Not far from the Basilica of St. John are the ruins (the

The impressive ruins of the Persecution Gate.

result of an earthquake) of the **Isa Bey Mosque**. The mosque was built in 1375 by Isa Bey, a Selçuk Sultan, surrounded by a high wall with three rows of finely fret-worked windows. An interesting highly decorated *portal* with numerous inscriptions leads into a courtyard where Turkish gravestones are displayed. The other side of the courtyard leads into the mosque which has a *prayer room* with pink and grey marble columns supporting the domes. One of these is decorated with a mosaic made from Turkey's famous ceramic tiles.

Ephesus should not be left without visiting its **Museum**, where items found during the excavations are shown. Some of these were removed from private dwellings, like the statues of Priapus and Eros, fragments of frescoes, friezes and fountains, There is also an interesting collection of Roman sculptures with busts of several emperors. In the room dedicated to the Goddess Artemis there are two towering statues facing each other, *Artemis the Great* and *Artemis the Beautiful*, which were discovered in the Prytaneion at Ephesus.

Four rows of protuberances hang from the Goddess's chest. In ancient times these were thought to represent breasts, then eggs and later testicles of bulls that had been sacrificed to the Goddess. Although Artemis was a virgin she was abundance incarnate, the Goddess of fertility and the protector of pregnant women.

Three items from the Museum at Ephesus: left, the statue of Artemis
Ephesia; right, a detail of the frieze from the Temple of Hadrian;
below, a resting warrior, a statue from the Ist century A.D.

The Gymnasium, a 3rd century Roman construction.

SARDIS

Sardis is an hour's drive from Smyrna. The site lies in fields of wheat, poppies and vines producing sultana raisins, much used in Turkish cuisine, but are also widely exported. Sardis was an important Lydian capital, founded on the banks of the famous gold-laden river Pactolus. Gold was Sardis's fortune and the fortune of its famous king Croesus who possessed immense treasures. It is said that his father Alyattes even invented coinage. Croesus's riches did not protect him from the Persians who conquered the kingdom in 574 B.C. After a period under Alexander the Great, Sardis became part of the Roman Empire and in the Book of Revelations St. John records that it was one of the seven churches.

The ruins can be seen by following the ancient road paved with marble slabs which leads to the remains of an imposing **Gymnasium**, built by the Romans in the third century on two floors with an interior court. The facade is decorated with fluted columns and has been recently restored. Next to the Gymnasium is an ancient **Synagogue** dating from the third century. It has a mosaic floor and the walls are panelled with marble and the marble altar is supported by four eagles. The **House of the Bronzes**, built in the fifth century and now a museum of religious articles, should not be missed. It was probably originally a priest's house. The **Temple of Artemis** rises up on a hill. It is an imposing building started by the Lydian king, Croesus, but it was never finished. Herodotus wrote that the king wished to use ten tons of gold in its construction. Later Alexander added eight columns to the facade and twenty on the sides. The Romans embellished it with statues of the married couple Antoninus Pius and Faustina and in 400 A.D. it even became a church.

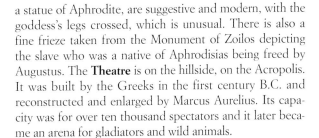

Aphrodisias lies one hundred and seventy kilometres from Kuşadasi, in the foothills of Mount Baba Daği not far from the village of Geyre by the river Maeander. In antiquity Aphrodisias was dedicated to the Goddess of beauty, love and sensuality, Aphrodite, who was worshipped as the city's patron as is testified by the remains of a temple dedicated to her in the first century B.C. It was a refined city of culture, popular with artists, writers and philosophers such as Alexander of Aphrodisias, an authoritative commentator on Aristotle or Chariton, who wrote erotic novels. The city was much loved by the Emperor Augustus who took an interest in its welfare and in his honour the citizens erected the **Sebasteion**, a slightly feminine, and the remains of the lower part of a statue of Aphrodite, are suggestive and modern, with the goddess's legs crossed, which is unusual. There is also a fine frieze taken from the Monument of Zoilos depicting the slave who was a native of Aphrodisias being freed by Augustus. The **Theatre** is on the hillside, on the Acropolis. It was built by the Greeks in the first century B.C. and reconstructed and enlarged by Marcus Aurelius. Its capacity was for over ten thousand spectators and it later became an arena for gladiators and wild animals.

Next to the theatre are the ruins of the **Baths of Hadrian**, an impressive building erected in the second century A.D. The marble flooring is in a perfect state of conserva-

Left, a detail of the Temple of Aphrodite; right, a basrelief from the same Temple.

street sanctuary complex with decorated columns.

Keman Erim, an American archaeologist of Turkish origin who oversaw the excavations at Aphrodisias, called it a *Graeco-Roman Florence*. Its origins date back to the bronze age, around 3,000 B.C. Its growth and prosperity began with the Greeks and continued with the Romans. In the fifth century under Leo I, it became Caria's capital and in the seventh century it was renamed Stavropolis, the City of the Cross. It became the see of a Bishopric, but Christianity came late to Aphrodisias, such was the people's deep-rooted attachment to the pagan goddess. The city was invaded by Selçuks and Ottomans and after being sacked by Tamerlane, it lost all spirit and was later abandoned.

Before entering the archaeological zone, visit the **Museum** which has a collection of sculptural treasures, Graeco-Roman statues and ceramics dating from the bronze age. The head of Apollo is breathtakingly ravishing, perfect and tion. The complex was made up of five different areas with a gymnasium with columns and two large pools. At the bath's entrance through the main gate there is a sinister door-knocker depicting the head of Medusa. The **Odeum**, or city meeting-place, had both stage and steps made of white marble. Not many of these survive as is the case with few fluted columns remaining in the **Temple of Aphrodite** behind the Odeum. The temple was built in the first century B.C. with a double columned structure and a cella and an atrium. Later Christians converted it into a basilica. Behind the sacrarium the spiral columns of the main entrance to the *Tetrapylon* can be seen. Through here pilgrims entered Aphrodite's sanctuary.

The **Stadium**, is a jewel of Graeco-Roman architecture. The architectonic oval is perfectly pitched so as to allow complete visibility. Thirty thousand spectators could fit into the twenty-two rows of steps.

Opposite, the remains of a temple at Aphrodisias.
Above, and on the following two pages, views of the extraordinary calcareous cascades and pools at Pamukkale.

PAMUKKALE - HIERAPOLIS

On the road to **Hiera-polis** you come across the extraordinary spectacle of **Pamukkale** or "**Cotton Castle**", unique for its cascades of lukewarm calcareous water, which drop after drop, and century after century have covered the walls of the mountain with lacework creating a kind of natural swimming pool. Here as dusk falls, the light is dazzling, creating a spectacle that is one of nature's marvels.

However Pamukkale is invaded by visitors not only for its beauty but for the therapeutic qualities of the water, celebrated since antiquity as being a cure for rheumatism and asthma.

There are still **Baths** at Hierapolis, on the hill above Pamukkale which have now become a museum. The ancient rooms serving as the *frigidarium* and the *caldarium* were clad in marble and had vaulted ceilings. In the **Museum** there is a collection of bronzes, glass and coins found during excavations and an unusual assortment of sculpture.

Near the remnants of a sixth-century Christian *basilica* with three naves are the foundations of a **temple to Apollo**, dating from the third century A.D. The recently restored second-century **Roman Theatre** is beautiful and majestic with fifty rows of travertine steps. The theatre is still in use when dances are performed during the city's much appreciated Festival.

Outside the walls is the **Martyrion of the Apostle Philip**, a fifth-century sanctuary with an octagonal chamber where it is believed that the saint was martyred in 87 A.D. The unusual **Arch of Domitian** with a triple arch flanked by two round towers should not be overlooked. It was erected by Julius Frontius, Proconsul of Asia, in honour of the Emperor during the first century A.D. Neither should the city's **Necropolis** be omitted. There are about one thousand tombs, some small and simple, some majestically sumptuous and impressive, dating from many different periods.

Left, a detail from the frieze of the Roman Theatre.
Below, the ruins of the beautiful Theatre at Hierapolis.

From time immemorial the sick and the moribund, rich and poor, have gathered here seeking the healing powers of the waters.

Those who died had waiting graves. Hierapolis, meaning "Holy City" was destroyed by earthquake on more than one occasion. It became a Bishopric see before becoming subject to the Turkish Selçuks; a final earthquake razed the city to the ground after which it was never rebuilt. One unusual detail is that the famous philosopher Antipater, who later became the Emperor Caracalla's tutor, was born here.

Right, a detail of the Necropolis at Hierapolis.
Below, the unusual Gate of Domitian, from the Ist century A.D.

A beautiful panorama of Kusadasi and the coast.

KUŞADASI

From being a village of fishermen and farmers **Kuşadasi** has recently become a sought-after holiday destination with fine sandy beaches and clean turquoise sea. It is crowded with tourists and yachts and caiques at anchor. It is a stepping-off point to visit historic sites nearby such as Ephesus, Priene or Didyma.

Kuşadasi has been long known as the "Island of the Birds", since herons, pigeons, doves and many other birds come here, in season, to nest. It is located on a beautiful bay near the Greek island of Samos, in the Aegean Sea.

In ancient times the Byzantines settled here and in the middle ages the Genoese, Venetians and Pisans came here to trade and renamed it Scala Nuova.

They built roads, a large port and a fortress which later became the refuge of the pirate Barbarossa and his two brothers for many years. He was the terror of the Mediterranean, looting and sacking ships and capturing sailors whom he sold as slaves in Istanbul's markets.

A small *mosque*, a splendid **caravanserai**, the *Öküz Mehemet Paşha Kervansaray*, now a luxury hotel, and the *Haman Kaleiçi* Baths all date from the Ottoman period.

Panorama of the ruins of the Temple of Athena, at Priene.

PRIENE

The origins of this beautiful city are old indeed. By the eleventh century B.C. it was one of the twelve colonies forming the Ionian Confederation and enjoyed considerable prestige and prosperity. It was situated below the mass of Samsum Daği (formerly Mikale) on the shore before the river Maeander silted up the port. Now the sea is fifteen kilometres away and the surrounding plains have become immense cotton plantations. The city rebelled against Persian domination under King Cyrus and in revenge the Persians razed it to the ground. New Priene was reborn under Alexander the Great in 330 B.C. and after countless struggles and invasions became a Roman province in 129 A.D. The city regained its prosperity under the Emperor Augustus in spite of having a population of only seven thousand. During the Byzantine reign it became a Bishopric. **Priene** became part of the Ottoman Empire in the fourteenth century. The streets of Priene are unusual in that they are all horizontal and vertical, parallel and perpendicular, like a chess board. However comfortable shoes are a must, especially for those wishing to reach the top where at one time the Acropolis stood. Now there are only ruins, but the view is spectacular and

The remains of the Theatre at Priene; in the foreground, a marble throne with lions' feet pedestals. Facing page, a panorama of the ruins of the Agora at Miletus.

well worth the effort. On the other hand, the **Theatre** is still in good condition although it is partly submerged in trees and vegetation. The theatre was originally Greek and built in the fourth century B.C. but it was altered by the Romans in the second century A.D. and its seating capacity increased to hold six thousand spectators. The wall of the stage, which has two storeys, faces a row of five marble throne-like seats resting on pedestals in the form of lions' feet surrounded by ivy leaves. Perhaps the theatre was also used for debates and political meetings.

Only five fluted Ionian columns survive from the original sixty-six of the great **Temple of Athena Polias**, erected by Alexander the great in 334 B.C. In the centre there was once a statue of Athena seven metres high rivalling in size

the famous statue by Pheidias in the Parthenon in Athens. By the temple the ruins of houses belonging to rich citizens or important dignitaries can be seen. They had numerous rooms facing onto interior courtyards.

The **bouleuterion**, the ancient senate was constructed in the second century B.C. with an enormous council chamber capable of holding six hundred and fifty people. Almost nothing remains of the **prytaneion**, the city's administrative building, only the great courtyard. The **stadium** dates from the second century B.C. and is one hundred and ninety metres long. At one time there was a portico of Doric columns. Under this loggia athletes could train when it rained, but it was also used as a meeting place for the general population of Priene.

MILETUS

Miletus, modern **Balàt**, is fifteen kilometres away from Priene. It is on a hillside surrounded by large rice-fields some way inland. In ancient times Miletus had four large ports at the mouth of the river Maeander at the head of the gulf of Latmus. Now the sea is far off, silted up by the river. It had trade links with countries on the Mediterranean, the Black Sea and the Sea of Marmara. Miletus was of the most powerful and important Greek metropolises in Asia Minor and was part of the influential Ionian Confederation. The city encouraged erudition and founded several schools attracting scientists, architects, philosophers and geographers. Western philosophy originated in Miletus and it as the native city of famous men such as Anaximenes, Hippodamus, Cadmus and Isidorus. The first coins were minted in this city, exact weight measures were established and the Phoenician alphabet perfected. From the results of excavations, it appears that Miletus was actually the Hittite settlement Millawanda and it was certainly a Mycenaean colony by the fourteenth century B.C. Miletus then fell into Persian hands and was razed to the ground. It was rebuilt in 479 B.C. by Hippodamus, the famous architect and in due course passed to the Romans. It began to prosper once more, new streets and monuments were constructed, and it was renamed Castrum Palatia. The Apostle Paul preached Christianity here and

The Theatre at Miletus. Facing page, the remains of the Temple of Apollo at Didyma.

the Emperor Justinian built city walls. The Venetians established commercial trading posts. In 1424, under Sultan Murat II, Miletus became a city of the Ottoman Empire but as the port silted up, caused by detritus brought down by the river Maeander, the city's decline began.

The **Roman Theatre** dating from the second century A.D. could hold twenty-five thousand spectators. The stage was decorated with exceptional sculptures and friezes and the facade was impressive, measuring one hundred and forty metres. Two columns on the top rows supported the imperial box. At the summit of the hill there are ruins of an ancient Byzantine fortress, the **bouleuterion**, the city's oldest surviving building, in the centre of the two agoras. It was constructed along the lines of a semi-circular theatre and was dedicated to King Antiochus IV. The southern agora, the largest of the two, dates from the third century B.C. There were porticoes

on both sides housing numerous shops. It was, in fact, the market place but is now completely overgrown.

Close by the agora is an exquisite mosque, the **Ilyas Bey Camii**, built in 1400 A.D. by Ilyas Bey, emir of the Mentese. The mosque has a square floor plan surmounted by a central dome but the minaret has collapsed. The decorations above the entrance door and the niche (*mihrab*) are highly elaborate. The **Baths of Faustina**, built around 150 A.D. and named after the wife of the Emperor Marcus Aurelius are in excellent condition. The walls of the *frigidarium* and the *calidarium*, fifteen metres high, are complete and there is a statue of a lion from whose mouth water spouted. Even the dressing rooms are still recognisable. The remains of the *Gymnasium* are worth seeing; there is a surviving courtyard and various rooms, probably used as the students' classrooms. The **Museum** houses a collection of artifacts found during excavations.

DIDYMA

Today **Didyma** is a small village close to the sea and praised by tourists and Turks on holiday for its golden sandy beaches. The sea however is not the only attraction for tourists, more so the ruins of the famous **Temple of Apollo**, a superb example of architecture dating from the Graeco-Roman period, and a sign of the grandeur of this area, outstanding for culture and art. Even before the arrival of the Ionians, Didyma was a holy place and its oracle was much feared and much attended. The Persian King Xerxes destroyed the temple in 480 B.C., and looted many of the statues and also removed its vast treasury, which owed its magnitude to the generosity of Croesus, King of Lydia. Alexander the Great decided to rebuild the temple after his victory over the Persians which had never been completely finished, and was still uncompleted under the Romans, probably on account of its enormous dimensions (one hundred and twenty metres long and twenty-four wide). Christianity put an end to pagan rites and festivals and prevented the temple from being completed. Indeed, in one atrium of the temple a basilica was built.

Traces remain of the temple's base and three Ionian columns standing twenty-five metres high are still upright, out of the original one hundred and twenty. There are also stones from the sacrificial altar and an antique fountain. The interior court, the pronaos and the steps leading to the sacrarium can all be identified. All around there are fragments of statuary such as the head of the Medusa, with snakes for hair and fangs for teeth, as she was transformed by Athena. Facing the temple there are a few steps from a second-century B.C. **stadium**, where games were held on Apollo's feast days. A long **Sacred Way**, with colonnaded porticoes, lead from Miletus to the sanctuary.

BODRUM

Opposite the Greek island of Kos, on a stupendous peninsula in the Southern Aegean rises the city of **Bodrum**, Halicarnassus in ancient times, the Carian capital and native city of the historian Herodotus. Bodrum is similar in air and colour to parts of Southern Italy with oddly-shaped whitewashed houses filled with flowers, mostly purple and fuchsia-coloured bougainvillaeas, oleanders and prickly-pears. The city has plenty of shops selling almost everything and there are numerous restaurants, hotels, nightclubs and cafés along the shore. Street vendors ply marine sponges, oranges and mandarins. Bodrum has been called the St. Tropez of Turkey, for its translucent sea, numerous bays and small ports. The city has barely 25,000 inhabitants who during the winter live off fishing, sponge collecting, boat building and agriculture. The famous wooden boats called caiques are made here.

In ancient times Bodrum was first under Persian rule, and later Greek. The city was conquered by Alexander the Great and destroyed. Later the Romans controlled Bodrum and they were followed by the Selçuks and the Turks and in 1492 the city fell to the Knights of St. John, sovereigns of Rhodes (the Knights of Malta) who built the massive **Castle of St. Peter**. The castle was constructed using stones from the Mausoleum and dominates the

The beautiful coast at Bodrum.
Facing page, a view of the sea from the town with the castle in the background.

town. It was equipped with an early powerful cannon, at the time a novel instrument of warfare.

Several museums now occupy the large rooms in the castle. In the *Chapel of the Knights Hospitaller* for example is the **Museum of Underwater Archaeology**, where relics from Greek, Roman and Phoenician ships found on the sea bed are displayed. There are a number of finds from the Mycenaean period in the *French Tower* and a collection of amphorae in the *Serpent's Tower*.

Not a great deal remains of the most important monument, the **Mausoleum**, which Pliny the Elder celebrated as one of the seven wonders of the world. It was built by Artemisia in memory of her loved husband Mausolus (hence the name mausoleum) in the centre of the town. It had a rectangular floor plan with thirty-six Doric columns and it was surmounted by a pyramid-shaped roof with a frieze depicting a four-horse chariot and two statues perhaps representing Mausolus and Artemisia. Only a few marble fragments can be seen today but there are several drawings and pieces of recently unearthed sculpture. The other findings are in the British Museum in London.

Before leaving Bodrum take a boat trip south to the **Black Island** (Karaada) where baths in orange mud may be enjoyed. The Turks claim great healing properties for them and afterwards you can wash in water which gushes from a plentiful hot spring in the grotto.

THE MOST REFINED CUISINE IN THE MEDITERRANEAN

The Turks proudly claim that their cuisine is the most refined in the Mediterranean and ranks third in the world, after the French and the Chinese. It certainly has a long tradition and over the centuries it has become enriched and refined to suit the delicate palates of the Ottoman sultans. It is said that even the Romans liked to employ Turkish cooks in their kitchens. Olive oil, butter, fragrant herbs and aromatic spices make up the base of Turkish cuisine and their recipes involve using high quality vegetables, fish and rice. Peppers and aubergines are prepared in hundreds of different ways.

Nomads were traditionally meat eaters, and the thin slices over Pide (a kind of pitta bread) moistened with melted butter, tomato sauce and yoghurt. This dish is almost always accompanied by a good glass of Ayran, a drink made with yoghurt and water and a good pinch of salt. Patlican Salatasi, a puree of aubergines is delicious as are Etli Dolma Içi, which are peppers stuffed with meat, rice and raisins from Sardis or Corinth.

The Turks attach great importance to Meze, mixed hors d'oeuvres, accompanied by piping hot pide and served on a round plate thirty centimetres in diameter. It make a meal on its own. Raki, an aniseed-flavoured spirit served in tall narrow glasses, should be drunk with Meze.

Above, a stall selling şiş kebab, delicious spit-roasted goat. In the large photograph, a fruit stall.

Turks eat mutton, lamb, goat and beef. Börek, pastry parcels filled with mince, cheese or fish which are then fried or cooked in the oven, are a tasty appetizer. The famous köfte meat croquettes come in many varieties and are dusted with aromatic spices. Sis kebab, charcoal-grilled chunks of goat, mutton or lamb with vegetables on a skewer are a daily staple.

Anatolia's traditional dish has a wonderful smell and an appetizing appearance. It is called Döner Kebab and it is an enormous roll of meat roasted on a vertical spit. It is served in When water is added to Raki, as it usually is, it becomes cloudy and opaque and the Turks call it Aslan sütü meaning Lions' Milk.

Turkish desserts are excellent and very sweet. Baklava, for example, is thin puff pastry filled with nuts and honey dipped in lemon syrup flavoured with orange blossom. Lokum, a traditional Turkish dessert, is made with sugar, cornstarch, dried fruit and spices. This dish was known in the fifteenth century, but was then made with honey instead of sugar and flour in place of cornstarch.

A view of the splendid bay of Marmaris.

MARMARIS

Marmaris is on a wide peninsula, in a bay with three small islands. It is a delightful place on the sea and the coast is full of mostly deserted hidden coves and inlets and all you need to discover them is a boat and the help of a fisherman. There are sandy beaches and the water is translucent and the colour of turquoise so that you can often see the sea bed. Marmaris is crowded especially in the summer, but many Europeans spend the winter here as it is quieter and more secluded than nearby Bodrum.

The growth of tourism in the last few years has transformed Marmaris from a fishing village into a comfortable holiday resort. The streets are wide and lined with trees, and not only palms: here plane trees and eucalyptus hold sway. There are numerous cafés, restaurants and entertainment places on the sea front. There are no ancient ruins at Marmaris although it has been identified as the site of ancient Physcus. There is only a castle and a caravanserai to see.

The **caravanserai**, on the road leading to the castle, was built in stone by Süleyman the Magnificent in 1545. It was meant to be occupied by Ottoman knights.

The **castle** was built in 1522, also by the Sultan Süleyman, as a base from which he could attack the island of Rhodes, the stronghold of the Knights of St. John. The bastions afford a splendid view of the sea and of Marmaris.

The remains of the Acropolis at Knidos, situated close to the sea.

KNIDOS

Knidos had a glorious past but the ruins that can be seen today bear no trace of its former splendour. However the bleak landscape and its position on the tip of the peninsula between two bays make it a wild but enchanting spot. Knidos was in existence by the seventh century B.C. and was inhabited by a colony of Spartans who traded with neighbouring countries by sea. The city then colonised the Lipari Islands and became part of the Dorian Confederation until it changed allegiance and formed an alliance with the Persians against Athens.

Knidos fathered some illustrious citizens such as Eudoxus, the mathematician, who was Plato's pupil and assistant, or Ctesias, the doctor and geographer who lived at the Persian Court, or Sostratus who designed the Pharos, the great lighthouse of Alexandria in Egypt. A School of medicine was established there in the fifth century B.C., the oldest hellenistic school of this nature. The inhabitants of Knidos worshipped Aphrodite, goddess of love and the sea, and Demeter, the goddess of fertility. Praxiteles sculpted a **nude statue of Aphrodite** and Pliny described it as the most beautiful statue in the world. The statue was placed on the altar in the circular temple of Aphrodite so that it could even be seen from the sea. Unfortunately there are no longer any traces of the temple. Parts of the Hellenic walls of the **Acropolis** are visible as are parts of the **Theatre** by the port. It was originally Greek, but modified by the Romans and the surviving areas are well preserved. Only a few stones are left of the fortifications.

A panorama of the stupendous Bay of Olü Deniz, near Fethiye.

FETHIYE

Modern **Fethiye** is none other than the ancient city of Telmessus, the Lycian city that worshipped a divinity named Kakasbos, identified with Heracles, to whom the city dedicated a temple. Five hundred years before Christ Telmessus was one of the most important cities of the Delian League.

Unfortunately most of the evidence testifying to the past has been destroyed by two violent earthquakes but even so Fethiye attracts more and more tourists each year, because the charm of this town of twenty-five thousand inhabitants lies not in its archaeological interest but in its natural setting. It is situated in one of the most attractive and romantic parts of the coast where nature has surpassed herself. Protected on the sides by forests of fir-trees and the Taurus chain of mountains, Fethiye lies on a bay on this jaggy coastline, dotted with creeks, rocky islands and two ports, one commercial and one for tourist traffic.

The city's most important monument is the craggy **Necropolis**. Amongst the many tombs dug out of the rock the most unusual is the monumental shrine of Amyntas (fourth century B.C.) in the form of a Greek temple with two Ionic columns.

Lycian tombs and sarcophaguses can be found all over Fethiye, by the roadside where lorries, cars and horses pass by indifferently. The Lycians did not bury their dead, but they built them tombs in the rocks, rather like nests, to assist the demons who, according to their religious beliefs, took on the form of birds to carry away the

souls of the dead and take them to the "light". Because of this Lycian tombs are also found at Kadyanda, the village of Üzümlü, near Fethiye.

A visit to the **bay of Ölü Deniz**, the "Dead or Calm Sea", only a few kilometres from Fethiye is almost obligatory. It is a paradisal natural oasis sheltered from the open sea, and stretches out towards the lagoon with its luxuriant vegetation and fine white sand.

The sea water changes colour from green, to blue and turquoise. Caiques, but not motor boats, are allowed to enter this enchanting place where one can bathe or fish underwater or walk in the park.

On these pages more views of the marvellous coast and the sea at Fethiye. On the side, a typical rock-cut tomb.

The famous fountain at the Letoon, with the nymphaeum which is now covered by water.

LETOON

Letoon was a Lycian city devoted to the worship of the Goddess Leto, the mother of Apollo and Artemis, and much loved by Zeus. Letoon is four kilometres from the city of Xanthus and in ancient times they were joined by a Sacred Way. The origins of the two cities, judging from archaeological finds, date from the eighth century B.C.

The city had **three temples** attracting pilgrims who followed the cult of the goddess. Some remains of these are still visible. The Temple of Apollo was built in the Doric style and has surviving mosaics; the Temple of Leto was Ionic. The oldest temple, dedicated to Artemis, was built between the two and dates from the fourth century B.C. In the small city museum's collection there is a famous stone trilingual stele bearing a decree from the Satrap of Lycia written in Aramaic, Lycian and Greek.

The renowned porticoed fountain, **the nymphaeum**, is now mostly covered by flood water that continually covers the land where numerous frogs maintain a noisy chorus from morning to night.

According to legend Leto wished Apollo and Artemis to drink from the fountain in the nymphaeum, but the citizens protested and so Leto transformed them all into frogs.

View of the steps of the Theatre at Xanthos, dating from the 2nd century B.C.

XANTHUS

The Lycian city of **Xanthus** lies a few kilometres inland from the sea, on a promontory which rises steeply from the river Kocaçay, the river Xanthus in antiquity, which marked the border with Caria. Legend has it that the city's founder was the hero Sarpedon, Hector's friend. Xanthus was destroyed by the Persians under their general Harpagus in the sixth century and it was later conquered by Alexander the Great in 333 B.C. before becoming the Lycian capital in 167 B.C. when it joined the Lycian confederation uniting twenty-three cities. Xanthus began to flourish and, under the Byzantines, became a Bishopric.

Not a great deal remains today to remind us of the city's past. There is a Roman Theatre, built on the site of an earlier Greek Theatre that dates from the second century B.C. but only a few steps and part of the stage wall survive. Next to the theatre, on the Acropolis, are the ruins of a **Byzantine basilica** that was looted and then destroyed by the Arabs and a **tomb on a pillar** bearing an inscription in Lycian, an Indo-European language that underwent transformation in Asia Minor.

The so-called **Harpy Tombs** (monsters with the bodies of birds and the faces of women) and the Nereid Monument were genuine masterpieces. Of the former only the base survives and of the latter the foundations. Their precious sculpted friezes are now in the British Museum in London.

The beach with fine white sand at Patara.

PATARA

Patara is on the Aegean Sea, and has a long, beautiful beach with fine, white sand. The sea is translucent and greeny-blue in colour. As on the beaches of nearby Dalyan, *Caretta* tortoises lay their eggs here. Patara is a magical place and even though they have been partially submerged by sand dunes, the ruins are evocative. Tradition recounts that the city was founded in the sixth century B.C. by Patarus, the son of Apollo. The city became the seat of the Roman Governors of Lycia and thrived off the port's commercial traffic, one of the most developed in the whole of Lycia in Roman times. The gradual silting up of the port caused Patara's slow decline. In times of antiquity the city was famous for its Oracle of Apollo, as respected as the Oracle at Delphi.

The ancient **triumphal arch** with three gates is well preserved and was erected in the first century B.C. by Mettius Modestus, the Roman Governor as the main entrance to the city. At either side of the arch there were marble statues of the Governor and his family.

The fairly large second-century B.C. **Theatre** is a spectacular sight because half the theatre had been buried by the sand and enormous olive trees have taken root on the steps of the other half. There are several **Lycian tombs** scattered about the ruins. There is a **Corinthian temple** by the small lake dating from the second century A.D. Its dimensions are modest but it retains a high wall and complete sculpted portal. On the other side of the lake the ruins of Emperor Hadrian's granaries can be seen. Grain stores were kept here before being dispatched from the port of Patara to the provinces of the Empire.

The marvellous beach at Kaş, on the same-named bay.

KAŞ

Kaş is situated on a beautiful bay where the Aegean Sea meets the Mediterranean. The crystalline seawater here is the colour of Iznik's painted tiles. There are small beaches with white pebbles here and there hidden in delightful creeks. Kaş is an ideal holiday destination and tourism has indeed exploded in recent years and more and more opulent yachts anchor in the port. However at Kaş it is still possible to enjoy sitting out in cafés by the sea front and to taste excellent *çay* (teas), apple or Rize tea, accompanied by large green and black olives.

Kaş is the ancient city of Antiphellus (founded by the Greeks and of great importance under the Romans) from where, according to Pliny the Elder, loads of wood from trees cut down in the Taurus forest would be shipped out of the harbour. It was also where fishermen found the finest sponges on the coast. Sponges are still found at Kaş but the town's more important activity is the manufacture and sale of gold and superb precious stones used in jewellery. The ancient **Theatre** of Kaş, of Greek origin, is in a fairly good state of repair with twenty-six rows of steps and a breathtaking view over the Mediterranean.

Tourists should not forget to see the large impressive *Lycian tomb* five metres high and dating from the fourth century B.C. located near the port. There are further rock-cut tombs on the rocky hillside above the city. At night, when the tombs are lit up, Kaş takes on an atmosphere of fabled magic. Before leaving Kaş visit the Greek island of Meis which was at one time Italian, or the **Mavi Mağara**, the Blue Grotto to see the suggestive reflections of light on the water.

The ruins of the ancient Byzantine Fortress of Kaleköy, on the island of Kekova.

KEKOVA

Kekova is an island on which there is much to see. It is long and thin and tongue-like, spanning the translucent sea. It is a quiet, restful paradise with plenty of creeks and bays. No other place is quite like it. Everywhere Roman and Byzantine friezes, fragments of statuary, ruins of churches and walls, and the remains of Lycian tombs can be seen under water in an extraordinary spectacle of submerged archaeology. Only a few people live on the island, most of them fishermen but they are friendly and will, for a small sum, guide you round the island. Do not miss tasting delicious fresh fish cooked on an open fire and enjoying the wonderful flavours of fire and sea.

There is a village on the island of Kekova dominated by a Byzantine fortress called **Kaleköy**, built on the site of ancient Simena. The small settlement of **Karaloz** and the **Bay of Tristomo**, where there are ruins of a Byzantine church can also be seen. There is a necropolis with tombs constructed like the hulls of upturned boats at **Teimiussa** by the modern village of **Üçağiz**.

MYRA - DEMRE

The archaeological site of ancient **Myra** is two kilometres away from modern Demre. The origins of this city date back to the fifth century B.C. The Lycians were an unified race, sharing coinage, a common language and script not dissimilar to Indo-European though Greek had replaced this language by the fourth century.

Myra flourished under the Romans and maintained its status as a free city. The city became the see of a Bishopric with St. Nicholas, who was consecrated Bishop here. The figure of St. Nicholas is much loved both by the Eastern and the Western churches on account of his association with Father Christmas. The story goes that one night the Bishop anonymously made donations of gifts and money contained in sacks which he lowered down chimneys. These were destined for poor girls who were unable to marry without sufficient dowries.

The **Church of St. Nicholas** was built in the third century A.D. It was later enlarged and embellished and, with the contributions made by pilgrims who came in ever increasing numbers, became a basilica. It is well preserved and was built with an atrium, an exonarthex, a narthex and three naves with apses. In the centre there is a dome decorated with frescoes that have now faded. The marble floor is in good condition and the Saint's tomb, which at one time contained his remains, is in the left nave. His body was removed in 1087 by Italian merchants, probably from Bari, where it was taken, and where it is still preserved today. They neglected to remove all the bones and those that were left behind can be seen in the museum at Antalya. Every year at Demre on December 6th a symposium is held in memory of St. Nicholas attended by the Church hierarchy and journalists. There is a well-maintained garden surrounding the church where a bronze statue of the heavily-bearded Saint, with a sack on his shoulders and accompanied by two children, looking indeed the very picture of Father Christmas, may be seen. In the city's **necropolis** there are tombs dug out of the rock, one next to another and these are the most fascinating monuments. They are highly decorated, with Graeco-Roman architectonic influences and look like real dwelling places. Some of them have bas-reliefs depicting family scenes with the deceased, others record the dead as they were when alive.

The stage is missing from the **Greek theatre**, built on the hillside, but its forty-seven steps are still in existence. There are a few evocative masks, carved in stone, scattered over the site.

The Greek Theatre at Myra. On the following pages, the rock necropolis and the monument to St. Nicholas at Demre, a place of pilgrimage on December 6th every year.

A view of the promontory of Phaselis, covered in luxuriant vegetation.

PHASELIS

Phaselis is situated on a promontory leading out to sea separating the city from Kemer by only twelve kilometres. There are sandy beaches there and luxuriant vegetation. Its ruins, mostly Greek and Roman have either been submerged or cut odd by the sea. The combination makes Phaselis a pleasant, romantic place. Phaselis was founded in the seventh century by colonists from Rhodes. It was a Lycian city and had three important ports which were in constant use, two of which were connected by a road lined with statues (some inscriptions can still be seen) and porti-coes where artisans worked and traded.

Alexander the Great spent considerable time at Phaselis; pirates made it their base for roaming the Mediterranean. In due course Phaselis became Byzantine and then, in 1150, it came under control of the Selçuk Turks. There are only a few surviving fragments of the mosaic floor from the ancient **Baths**. The theatre, now surrounded and immersed in vegetation, was originally Greek, and even the fine Roman aqueduct presents a romantic picture as it has been literally embraced by pine trees.

KEMER

Kemer, on the attractive Turkish Riviera has become a popular holiday destination in a very short time. It has numerous tourist villages adequately equipped for holidays but it has lost some of its Oriental Turkish atmosphere that at one time gave it character.

The city, founded around the second century B.C., is well worth a visit, not only to see its scanty ruins, but for its fantastic position on the sea. It has a sandy beach along both banks of a river hemmed in by rocks which leads straight down to the sea. In the past it was used as

Panorama of the Gulf of Kemer, showing its wonderful position.

Kemer has a splendid situation in an half-moon bay facing the Mediterranean with the pine-forested Taurus mountain chain (Beydağlari) as a backdrop.

The streets of Kemer are dotted with high palm trees, cafés, carpet dealers and workshops making leather goods. It is crowded with street sellers with all kinds of wares, from sesame buns, fresh or dried fruit to any kind of cigarettes.

A thirty-minute bus ride from Kemer brings you to ancient **Olympus**, the Lycian city where Mithras, the God of Fire, was worshipped.

a refuge by pirates.

The torrential river dries up in the summer but at other times it is used to clean the locally-made carpets.

A monumental portal and a small theatre curiously covered by fig trees, cacti and greenery are all that survive of Olympus's glorious ancient history.

A mule track up the mountainside leads to the **Chimaera**, a large rock that juts out from the mountain where a perpetual fire endlessly burns. The site recalls Homer's mythological narrative of Bellerophon and Pegasus, the winged horse.

The Theatre at Arycanda in a splendid valley surrounded by leafy mountains.

ARYCANDA

The ancient Lycian city of **Arycanda**, near the modern village of Çatallar and only thirty miles from the sea at Finike, took its name from the river Arycandos. Arycanda is situated high up, on the small mountain of Akdağ, and indeed its monuments were all constructed on terraces cut into the mountainside. The site is immersed in a wonderful landscape of spruce and above all pine trees.

Archaeological excavations, which are still in progress, have uncovered monuments that have withstood the passage of time fairly well. In ancient times Romans chose this city for their holidays, leaving the heat of the coast for the cooler temperatures higher up. Its origins date back to the fifth century. It was taken by the Persians and reconquered by Alexander the Great. On his death it was governed for a long time by the Seleucid Kings of Syria. Arycanda was a member of the Lycian confederation before forming part of the Roman Empire.

There were many rooms in the high-walled **Baths**. In the **Tepidarium** the flue allowing hot air to escape can be clearly seen.

In the **Necropolis**, not far from the Baths, there are many tombs in the shape of small temples, and highly ornate sarcophagi. From there a stairway leads to the best preserved monument, the **Theatre**. It is a superb example and splendidly situated between the mountains and the trees with a high stage wall and twenty rows of steps.

The **stadium** was constructed on the highest terraces of the mountain and the foundations of an ancient temple can be seen in the **Agora**.

The remains of the Theatre at Termessus, built in the Hellenistic period on the mountainside.

TERMESSUS

Termessus was built at an altitude of a thousand metres. It is an attractive city, isolated in the Mountains of Taurus. Getting there is quite tiring, but well worth the effort. The view from the top is unparalleled and compensates for the hike as on crystal-clear days you can see the sea, and, in the distance, Antalya.

Termessus is a Hellenic city but had been inhabited by the Psidians, a quarrelsome people who lived off the land by farming and sheep-rearing. They managed to fortify their city so effectively that they were able to withstand Alexander the Great's attacks, and after a friendly truce with the Roman Empire, Termessus was declared "a free city". Monuments and statues were built and the city enjoyed a certain affluence.

Christianity was practised here, and there was a church, but no trace has survived.

The most important ruins at Termessus are those of the **Necropolis**. Earthquakes have opened up the tombs and scattered them down the mountainside in macabre confusion provoking mixed feelings of revulsion and attraction. Of particular interest are the **Tomb of Lions** and the **Tomb of Alketas**, in the form of a Lycian dwelling, reserved for one of Alexander the Great's courageous generals.

The Hellenistic **Theatre**, built on the mountainside, held four thousand spectators on twenty-six rows of steps. The Romans enlarged it and made improvements. Only a gate testifies to the grandiosity of what was once the ancient *temple of Hadrian*. Huge water *cisterns*, ten metres deep were constructed on the mountainside and demonstrate an extraordinary engineering ability for that time.

Panorama of Antalya, thought to be one of Turkey's best holiday destinations on the Aegean Sea.

ANTALYA

Antalya was founded by Attalus II and named Attaleia in his honour. It is a splendid city by the sea, considered to be the finest on the Turkish Riviera on the Aegean, and it is called the "pearl" of the Turkish coasts. It is built on a promontory in a spectacular bay with the mountains of Taurus behind. It is a lively, festive place with a Mediterranean atmosphere, rich in vegetation, where the sun shines on the clear blue water of the sea. Even in the winter European tourists come here to spend the season in a paradise where cold and fog are unknown.

With more than a million inhabitants, Antalya lives off agriculture and small industry but most of all from tourism. On the fertile plain sugar cane, apricots and figs (some of which are dried) are grown and there are crops of oranges, bananas, mulberry trees and sweet green melons.

The best jams in Turkey can be found here, especially the ones made from bergamot and bitter oranges.

Hotels, pensions, boarding houses, restaurants, cafés and discotheques have opened at a terrific rate during the last fifteen years. The old port has been reconstructed and a new port built to cater for the ever growing numbers of pleasure boats. The beaches, whether pebbled or with fine sand, are spacious and along the sea front, lined with palms and plain trees, boutiques and sophisticated shops catering for European tastes can be found in plenty.

Roses are cultivated in Antalya, as they were in the past, the flower dear to the Islamic religion. There are large fields growing coloured roses and in the shops, even souvenir shops, you can buy perfumes, bars of soap and bottles of rosewater. Rose petals are dried and worked in the neighbouring city of Isparta. Antalya is divided between the new town with large modern buildings, and the old city, which is much more interesting, with the old Roman port, the old bazaar with tiny alleyways crammed with

jewellers, carpet dealers, scent and spice sellers and the characteristic Ottoman houses built of wood and brightly painted. Some of these have been turned into hotels, others restored and some are still abandoned. Restaurants serve delicious fish soups, stews, and quantities of grilled fish, washed down with Raki.

From Antalya excursions to cities nearby can be easily made. Some are rich in antiquities and excavations like Side, Perge or Aspendus. Or there are boat trips to see the waterfalls at Düden or the neighbouring islands or to the many romantic, hidden bays that can only be reached with the help of local fishermen.

The city, founded by Attalus II, King of Pergamum, was bequeathed to the Romans in 45 B.C. Later, under the Romans -when Hadrian, who visited the city, was Emperor - it became the capital of the Roman Asiatic province. The inhabitants, in gratitude, dedicated a splendid gate to the Emperor.

Antalya then became Byzantine and a new circle of walls was built to defend the city from the Arabs' continuous attacks. For a century, during the Crusades, Antalya became a naval base before succumbing to the Selçuk Turks. In 1391 it was annexed by the Sultan Beyazit I,

and became part of the Ottoman Empire.

The city is dominated by the **Yivli Minare**, the Selçuk minaret erected in 1230 with a fluted conical spire that was once decorated with majolica. It has become the city's symbol. By its side stood a **Byzantine church** that was transformed into a **mosque by Aladdin** in 1373. It has six domes and has become a cultural centre for exhibitions and conferences.

Hadrian's Gate is Antalya's most important and elegant antique monument. It was built of white marble with three arches with Corinthian columns and capitals and erected, as earlier mentioned, in 130 A.D. following the Emperor's stay in the city.

Between Hadrian's Gate and the second-century A.D. **Tower of Hidirlik**, fourteen metres high and formerly used as a lighthouse, is the **Kesik Minare**, the minaret mutilated during the **Ulu Camii** Selçuk period, that is now a ruin. It was built over a fine fifth-century Byzantine church with three naves dedicated to the Virgin Mary. In 1896 a fire destroyed the church and the upper part of the minaret which had been constructed in wood.

Not far from the Yivli Minare is the great **Antalya Museum**, which opened in 1972. In the garden there is a café with tables in the open air and a bookshop ensconced among fragments of sculpture and friezes.

The elegant, impressive Gate of Hadrian, Antalya's most important monument.
Opposite, the splendid Düden waterfalls. A popular place to visit by boat.

There are twelve rooms in the museum which has a wide-ranging collection of exhibits from fossils dating from the stone and bronze ages to Mycenaean statuettes and articles from the Hellenistic-Roman-Byzantine periods.

There some particularly fine statues of the Roman Emperors, Trajan, Hadrian, and Septimus Severus, and sarcophagi depicting the Twelve Labours of Hercules.

The museum also houses some of St. Nicholas's bones, those that the Italians failed to carry away. There are some interesting mosaics, frescoes and Byzantine icons with a particular attractive one depicting Jesus Christ with the Twelve Apostles.

*Left, a glimpse of an alleyway in the oldest part of the city.
Below, one of rooms of Antalya's Museum which
opened in 1972. Facing page, a panorama of Antalya, showing
the Yivli Minare, the Selçuk minaret erected in 1230.*

Panorama of the Theatre at Perge.
Facing page, the Hellenistic Gate, from the 3rd century B.C. with the ruins of its characteristic two round towers.

PERGE

Perge is an exceptionally ancient Greek city in Pamphylia and it appears to have been founded by Greek colonists from Troy who came here after their own city had been destroyed in the war. At one time Perge was connected to the sea via the navigable river Aksu (formerly Kestros). The ruins are splendid and bear witness to the bygone grandeur of this city. The city was enlarged in the second century B.C. under the dominion of Alexander the Great. The cult of the Goddess Artemis, "Queen of Perge", practised by the inhabitants, attracted visitors from all over Pamphylia. One of the fathers of mathematics, Apollonius, was born in Perge; the Apostles Paul and Barnabas preached here and the city became a centre of Christianity. Under Byzantium it became a Bishopric, but began to decline as a result of numerous Arab invasions.

The **Theatre**, built on the hillside at the time of the Emperor Trajan had thirty-eight rows of steps and could hold more than fifteen thousand spectators. The stage walls, now restored, were decorated with sculptures depicting the deities. A few panels of these bas reliefs are still visible. Facing the theatre is Perge's masterpiece, the **Stadium** - the best preserved in Asia Minor. It is two hundred and thirty-four metres long and thirty-four wide and dates from the second century A.D. It was constructed using arches to support the higher rows of steps allowing numerous shops to trade in the arcades below.

The third-century B.C. **Hellenistic Gate** is still today Perge's most important Greek monument, marked by two round towers at the roadside. Behind these were two apses with arched niches. These structures were the gift of Plancia Magna, the high-priestess of Artemis who also gave the city of Perge numerous statues.

The gate opened on to the famous **Colonnaded Way** that led to the **Acropolis**. Twenty metres wide, the street had porticoes on both sides which provided dwellings, shops and workshops.

Some of the recently-restored columns bear inscriptions visible today; the others were lost in a violent earthquake which also destroyed the nymphaeum, the fountain built at the time of the Emperor Hadrian. Finally the **Baths**, also recently restored, are perhaps the most beautiful in the whole of Turkey. There are numerous rooms with floors in fine condition and splendid marble pools.

Detail of the Theatre at Aspendus.
Facing page, above, an aerial view of ancient Perge; below, the ruins of the fountain situated north of the city.

ASPENDUS

Aspendus is fifty kilometres inland from the Antalyan sea, not far from the village of Belkis. The ruins of this city are Roman, with the exception of the bridge over the river Eurymedon which dates from the Selçuk period. However the origins of Aspendus are much earlier and date from one thousand years before Christ during the Hittite period. Aspendus became a Greek colony and was one of the more important cities in Pamphylia. In the fifth century it allied with the Persians and became rich through trading in horses, silk and carpets. Alexander the Great conquered the city and after a period under the Pergamum Kings it became part of the Roman Empire in 133 B.C. Today only ruins remain of the magnificent buildings erected by the Romans at Aspendus, except for the **theatre** very well preserved. Even General Atatürk himself was charmed by this theatre and its acoustics and had it restored. It is in use today for sporting and musical events.

The theatre is a testimonial to the grandeur of Roman architecture. It was designed by the architect Zeno (born at Aspendus according to the inscriptions over the two main gates) in the second century A.D. during the reign of the Emperor Marcus Aurelius. The theatre, built on the side of a hill, is semicircular and ninety-five metres wide, and it could seat over twenty thousand spectators on forty rows of steps. An exceptionally fine arcaded *gallery* surrounds the upper part of the cavea. The majolica *decorations* on some parts of the stage were added during Selçuk restorations. The Ottomans used the theatre as a caravanserai. A further example of Roman architecture is the first-century A.D. **Aqueduct**. It is nine hundred and twenty-four metres long, entirely arcaded and had two large cistern towers at each end.

On the top of the hill, in the Acropolis, are the ruins of a *nymphaeaum*, a *basilica* and a *fountain*.

Aspendus with the Ist century A.D. aqueduct. Below, the Selçuk Bridge over the river Eurymedon.
Facing page, the Theatre.

An aerial view of Side with the Theatre. Opposite, an evocative illustration showing the Temple of Apollo by night.

SIDE

Greek colonists from Aeolia founded the splendid city of **Side** in the seventh century B.C. and built a great seaport. A few decades ago Side was a peaceful fishing village but it has become a town of hotels, pensions and restaurants and its two thousand inhabitants live on and for tourism. In ancient times, like the Hellenes, Side became rich with money deriving from piracy and from the slave trade. Under the Romans these illicit activities ceased but the city remained fairly prosperous through commerce and traffic though its port.

During the Byzantine Empire Side became an important centre for Christianity, becoming a Bishopric; and the city was given the title of the Metropolitan Church for Eastern Pamphylia.

But Side is also famous as being the place where Anthony and Cleopatra met clandestinely for romantic assignations prior to their marriage.

Its decline began with attacks by the Arabs: the citizens abandoned the town and at the end of the fourteenth century Side became Ottoman.

The theatre at Side was one of the largest in Pamphylia, holding fifteen thousand spectators. It was built by the Romans in the third century A.D. on the plain, facing the sea. It was later re-inforced by the Romans, able engineers, with strong arch structures.

The museum is small but interesting, and has been installed amongst the ruins of the **Roman Baths**. It houses a collection of statues, friezes and sarcophagi found during excavations.

Outside the Hellenistic walls are the ruins of a **Byzantine basilica** that had three naves, a baptistery and the **Bishop's palace**. There were two agoras at Side, one of which was called the *State Agora* and used for meetings and public ceremonies.

The well-preserved Theatre at Side. Below, an aerial view of the coast.

Panoramic view of Alanya, a pretty town on the so-called "Turquoise Coast".

ALANYA

Alanya, in Southern Turkey, is an attractive city on the Riviera on the so-called "turquoise coast". It is built on a promontory of reddish earth, right over the sea and it is surrounded by two large sandy beaches and the sea front is full of hotels, cafés and restaurants. It is said the Queen Cleopatra so loved walking on the fine sand and to bathe in the clear blue water that Anthony presented her with this province. Alanya is an ideal city for holidays, being comfortable and elegant and it has numerous gardens and tree-lined street and avenues. Above all it has a wonderful climate, even in winter. The people are polite and friendly and on the streets women and children offer fragrant lemons and the sweetest bananas for sale. It is not by chance that Alanya is one of Turkey's more important centres for fruit and vegetables. The vegetation is luxuriant and there are endless orchards growing fruit, vegetable and bananas, and great forests of Aleppo pines growing to a height of twenty metres and woods with cedars of Lebanon.

The cuisine at Alanya is fairly good, specialising in "grilled mutton croquettes", and vegetable stews as well as charcoal-grilled fresh fish.

Alanya was named Coracesium by the Hellenes who founded the city, then pirates established their lair here for many years. One of these was the slave merchant, Diodotus Tryphon, who was tortured and killed by the Romans. Alanya, like the rest of Turkey, was to come into contact with many different civilisations, but here the Selçuk Turks, a nomadic race of Asiatic origin with exceedingly ancient traditions, customs and culture were the most influential. They differed from the Ottoman Turks who had Arab characteristics and who passed on the traditions of Islam.

The **Kizil Kule**, a massive, octagonal red tower thirty-five metres high, which dominates the harbour and the sea is a five-storeyed fortress. It now houses the Ethnographical Museum, displaying objects in daily use some dating from the Selçuks' nomadic period, as well as carpets and antique looms. There is an exceptional view from the crenellated bastions at the top of the tower.

The **Selçuk Tersane**, the old naval dockyard is well preserved with five jetties, roof and arcades built of red brick and a marble gate. It is still in use today for minor caulking repairs.

An impressive **Citadel** looks down over the town with a fortress, water cisterns and the ruins of the old Sultans' Palace. There are also the remains of a fine Byzantine church, dedicated to St. George, in the Citadel. It has retained vaults and arches on the exterior and there are faded frescoes in the dome. On the highest part of the rock, and the spot is not difficult to locate, prisoners condemned to death were thrown into the sea.

But Alanya's masterpiece are the massive walls surrounding the city. They are eight kilometres long, crenellated, with numerous intervening rectangular towers that are forts in themselves.

Alanya's colourful market is cheerful and amusing, bustling with people. All kinds of material can be bought here, from silk to cotton and linen. There are attractive and unusual bathing wraps in gaudy colours. You can also find small handmade leather objects and other crafts. The old covered Bedesten is in the old part of Alanya, hidden amongst the stone houses and alleyways and buried under fig trees and other greenery.

Delightful trips to grottoes nearby can be made by boat. The fishermen are well disposed and for a small sum they are happy to accompany tourists who wish to see the romantic lovers' grotto, **l'Aşiklar Mağarasi**, or the evocative **Fosforlu Mağarasi** where the stony bottom of the blue sea seems to be phosphorescent.

Right, a corner of the beach at Alanya.
Left, a panoramic view of the impressive fortress, situated in a dominant position overlooking the sea.

Panorama of the city with the Alaeddin Camii in the foreground.

KONYA

Konya or **Iconiensum** is a city with eight hundred thousand inhabitants situated at an altitude of over one thousand metres in the Anatolian steppe. It is surrounded by an immense plateau where wheat, poppies, cotton and fruit trees are farmed. Konya is the "Granary of Turkey". The city is one of the oldest in the world, indeed Çatalhöyük, the nearest village, was a settlement by 7,800 B.C. Doorless mud houses and stone objects and instruments for daily use have been excavated there and are now displayed in the Anatolian Museum at Ankara.

Konya is an unusual, though traditional city. Splendid European tree-lined boulevards have been built where once the city's walls stood, and there is a prestigious sought-after university. This Turkish city is deeply religious and rigorously observes the Koran and is known as a "Holy City" where the women are veiled. The city is a place of continuous pilgrimage for the Muslim faithful being the homeland of *Sufism*, which was spread from Konya by the Persian mystic poet Mevlana.

The origins of this city - an oasis in the steppe - are, as we have mentioned lost in antiquity. Many civilisations took root here, beginning with the Hittites (4,000 B.C.) who named the place *Kuwanna*, to the Phrygians, Assyrians, Lydians, Persians, Romans, Seleucids, Arabs and Selçuks, before it too finally succumbed to the Ottoman Empire. Under the Romans Konya enjoyed a fair degree of prosperity and was named Claudiconium, after the Emperor Claudius. The Apostles Paul and Barnabas preached the

The Monastery-Mausoleum of Mevlâna with its conical dome decorated in green majolica, showing on the left the Selimiye Camii.

Gospel here and converted the city to Christianity which later, under the Byzantines, became a Bishopric. In 1097 Konya became a capital under Selçuk rule and managed to repel attacks from the crusaders and Frederick Barbarossa. The city reached its zenith under the Sultan Alaeddin Keykubat in 1219 who had spent long years in exile at the Byzantine court and had absorbed its profoundly Western nature. He erected strong city walls, beautified the town with palaces and mosques and gave hospitality at court to artists, scientists and philosophers such as Jalal ad-Din ar-Rumi, known as Mevlana, who founded the order of the **Dancing Dervishes**.

Before attending to the monuments and masterpieces of art, visitors should immerse themselves in the atmosphere of the "historic centre" of the town, where one can breathe in the history and the spirit of that noble, refined race, the Selçuks, who are the real founders of this city.

Almost nothing remains from the Roman and Byzantine period, except forty-two columns with capitals supporting the wooden roof of the **Alaeddin Camii**, the Selçul mosque (now being restored) and constructed in 1220 and which is a perfect example of Arab architecture. It is situated high up on a hill, on the site of the former Acropolis, and is now surrounded by the luxuriant vegetation of a well-maintained park. However, from Alaeddin's Palace a fine marble portal has survived.

The old School of Theology, the **Büyük Karatay Medresesi** dating from 1251 which has an impressive and splendidly decorated marble portal, is now a **Museum of Ceramics** with a collection of Selçuk majolica.

The **Ince Minare Medresesi**, the Medrese of the Slender Minaret, also possesses an ornate ceramic portal and the building houses an unusual museum with a collection of wooden and stone sculpture. Its minaret, six hundred

The interior of the Monastery-Mausoleum of Mevlâna with the sarcophagus of the Persian Celaleddin Rumi.
Left, a panorama of the suggestive salt lake (Tüz Golü).

years old, which gives its name to the building, was damaged by lightning a hundred years ago and was never repaired. The **Mevlana Monastery**, with its characteristic conical dome, entirely faced in green ceramics, was once the monastery of the Dancing Dervishes. It now houses a **Museum of Islamic Art** which has a collection of precious manuscripts, antique carpets and musical instruments. Inside you can see the **Mevlana Turbesi**, the burial place of the Sufist Jalal ad-Din ar-Rumi and his followers, a place of great importance for the cult.

Leaving Konya stop and look at the great salt lake (saltier than the Black Sea) called **Tüz Golü** which in the summer dries up and covers more than a hundred kilometres with salt. It is completely white, an extraordinary sight extending further than the eye can see.

DANCING FOR ECSTASY

The Dance of the Dancing Dervishes is one of the most original performances a tourist can see in Turkey. Its history is very ancient.

Celaleddin Rumi Mevlâna, a poet, philosopher and mystic of Afghan origin, lived for a long time in mony and start the dance (samà). The dervishes wear long white dresses symbolising the shroud and their great black cloaks represent the tomb and their red conical hats the tomb stone. The soul is darwish, (poor) and so the dervish is poor, and we

The celebrated "Dancing Dervishes", in their typical movements of whirling and spinning around.

Konya where he had been invited to teach in the School of Islamic Theology by the Selçuk Sultan, Alaeddin Keykubad.

He soon abandoned teaching and took up meditation. His most known writings are the Mesnevi and the Divan el Kebir, a collection of poetry in Persian, then the court language under the Selçuks, and later translated into Turkish. Mevlâna's doctrine, whose principal tenet was the centrality of God, preached tolerance, understanding and compassion. He advocated monogamy and condemned the practise of slavery.

Mevlâna, whose name means Our Lord, adored music and dancing and he used them as instruments to entrust himself completely to God and to God's love. The Mavevli, or band of "Dancing Dervishes" was assembled after the death of Mevlâna by his son, the Sultan Veled.

The dance has three successive phases: the first concerns the knowledge of God, the second the vision of God and the third union with God. The sweet notes of the reed flute (ney) initiate the cere- are all poor with the exception of God, in the words of the muslim chant. This is the beginning of the sacred cosmic dance of the dervishes who start to spin round on themselves. At the third turn they drop their cloaks, a symbol that they have lost their worldly troubles. Then, still spinning, they hold out their right hands and raise the palms of their hands upwards so they can receive the blessing and grace from heaven which will also reach their left hand, open and reaching for the ground. Spinning faster and faster, the dancers' ample white dresses rotate in an ideal representation of the movement of the celestial spheres around God. In this way the dancers achieve ecstasy.

These dances are frequently performed for tourists, and it is also possible to see them at a festival that takes place at Konya between December 14th and December 17th every year. In 1925 Kemal Atatürk proclaimed the secular, democratic Republic of Turkey and dissolved the fraternity of the Dervishes, who originally were entrusted with converting Christians in Anatolia to Islam.

A view of the remains of the Roman aqueduct, near Silifke.

SILIFKE

Silifke is a modern town of twenty-five thousand inhabitants. Built on a fertile plain at the mouth of the river Göksü (Calycadnus) where Frederick Barbarossa drowned at the command of the Third Crusade. Silifke was the ancient city of Seleucia, founded by Seleucus I Nicator. Under the Roman Empire the city became one of the richest cities in Cilicia. After many years under Byzantium, Silifke was annexed by the Ottoman Empire.

Not a great deal of the city's past remains. The most fascinating monument is the **Castle-fortress**, a mighty construction dominating the city from the hillside. It dates from the medieval Byzantine period but was disfigured by the Crusaders around the twelfth century. It was built on the site of Seleucia's acropolis. From the castle the ruins of a large **Roman cistern**, excavated in the rock, can be seen.

A few fluted columns with Corinthian capitals testify to the **Temple of Zeus**. Silifke's Ulu Camii, the Selçuk mosque, has retained its fine door and the mihrab. There is a collection of coins, Graeco-Roman sculpture dating from the fourth to the second century B.C. and numerous objects in silver, glass and bronze in the **Archaeological Museum**.

Leaving Silifke, the ruins of the basilica of St. Thecla can be glimpsed. The three-naved basilica was constructed around 476 A.D. by the Emperor Zeno above a grotto where the saint, whose name in Turkish is Ayatekla, hid after she had miraculously escaped from being burned to death. In the interior of the grotto there are several rooms with arched ceilings and columns. The surroundings of Silifke are of great interest. Twenty kilometres away is **Corycus**, an important trading post in the past for Venetian and Genoese commerce. Three small churches have been built in the **castle of Corycos**, a twelfth century construction erected by an Armenian prince. Inside the churches frescoes are still visible, although they have faded with time. On a small island facing the city is the **Virgins' Castle**, built by the Armenian king, Leo II. A small but elegant church can be seen in the courtyard.

The splendid waterfalls on the river Kydnos, near the town of Tarsus.

TARSUS

Tarsus is known throughout the world as the birthplace of St. Paul, the Apostle. It is now a small congenial town of two hundred thousand inhabitants living off industry and agriculture. It is the only town in the whole of the Mediterranean to have kept its original name for more than three thousand years. This was a Cilician city, built on the banks of the river Kydnos (now called Tarsus Suyu) and surrounded by a vast plain. In the covered bazaar, the Kirk Kasik, beautifully made linen and cotton fabrics can be bought at minimal cost.

In our memory Tarsus evokes the Apostle Saul, who became Paul after his conversion who, Tarsus-born, tried to bring Christianity to Anatolia. But the city is also remembered in history for one singular occasion: it was the scene of the romantic encounter between Mark Anthony and Cleopatra, Queen of Egypt. As Plutarch relates in his "Life of Anthony", Mark Anthony was transfixed by the Queen's beauty. Cleopatra reached the city by ship - at that time the river was still navigable - and appeared as a vision of Venus. Tarsus has ancient origins indeed; from 3,000 years before Christ up to the fourteenth century B.C. it was a Hittite city and became Dorian around 1,200 B.C. Alexander the Great conquered it in 333 B.C. and the Seleucids made it a centre of culture. After the devastation caused by the Armenian king, Tigranes the Great in 94 B.C., Tarsus came under Roman rule in 64 B.C. For two years the city was governed liberally by Cicero. The Romans built a canal connecting the city to the sea, creating a commercial city with a port.

The Byzantines ruled for a long time in Tarsus, a city privileged by its geographical position. In fact, as well as the navigable river, it possessed the Gate of Cilicia (or the Gate of Judas), a military artery giving access across the mountains of Taurus to Mesopotamia and Syria. At the city's entrance there is a Roman Gate, known as **Cleopatra's Gate** or the **Gate of St. Paul**. Over the *Armenian Church of St. Peter*, a fine example of structural and dimensional harmony, the **Kilise Camii** mosque rises today. On the site of *St. Paul's Basilica*, another great sixteenth-century mosque, the **Ulu Camii**, was erected.

From the ancient **St. Paul's Well**, certainly of Roman origin, water can still be drawn today. It was so named because it is in the Jewish quarter of the town.

Before leaving Tarsus altogether, make an agreeable detour to view the **waterfalls** of the river Kydnos, which can be found by the ruins of an ancient Roman dam, preferably while sitting drinking coffee in the ramshackle Turkish-style bar, facing the water.

THE HAMAM: A RITUAL GUARDED FOR CENTURIES

For centuries a Turkish bath has been a magical, hygienic, religious rite, a culture that has been carefully handed down. Men and women are rigorously separated in the hamam which were built all over Turkey, wherever Islam had spread. It was indeed the Islamic religion which adopted the Roman heritage of bathing in sumptuous highly-decorated buildings with marble furnishings and spectacular architecture, enjoying massages, oils, fragrant perfumes and invigorating steam.

Inside designated cabins, once undressed, your body is wrapped in a cloth and you pass from the cold room to the tepid room, then to the hot room where you relax while sweating in the scented steam. An energetic masseur wearing a coarse glove then massages your whole body, helping you to get rid of toxins, toning

values. It is written in the Koran that no prayer has any worth in the eyes of God unless the body is pure and cleansed. Hence the hamam are never far from mosques.

Tourists should go to the "Turkish Baths" and relish the benefit and the culture of the bath, which is an unforgettable experience, completely different from the hygienic saunas in Europe. Even the most forgotten village in the Anatolian steppe has its hamam. In Istanbul alone there are a hundred, such as the famous Cagaloglu Hamani a few steps from Santa Sofia, built during the reign of Süleyman the Magnificent and frequented by King Edward VII and the Emperor William II. The Eski Kaplica at Bursa, built on the site of ancient Roman baths, are thought to be the most beautiful in Turkey.

The pleasures of the turkish bath.

your muscles and resuscitating the sleepy parts of your body. The bath ends with a rinse first in hot water, then in cold. Next, wrapped up in a towel, conviviality begins over a cup of apple tea, simple Turkish tea or coffee. In fact the hamam are also meeting places for business, conversation or socialising. According to Turkish culture the bath regenerates and heals the body and the soul and therefore has social

At one time, entrance to the baths was free, with no distinctions of class, also because no private house had large baths or sanitation. Today you buy an entrance ticket and if you want a massage it is a good idea to agree a price beforehand. Turkish women would never agree to be massaged by a man, even if he was the best, but it is acceptable for foreign women.

A nocturnal panorama showing Adana's thousand lights.

ADANA

Adana is Turkey's fourth largest city with a population of one million two hundred thousand inhabitants. It is the capital of Cilicia and has grown rapidly in the last few years. It used to be an agricultural community surrounded by a fertile plain but it is now an industrial city concerned with fabrics and oil refining. Tourism has developed, and more hotels open each year and its universities are well attended. Hittites settled at Adana in the fifteenth century B.C. and then the Greeks founded an important colony. It was later invaded and conquered by the Assyrians, then by Antiochus IV Epiphanes. It then became Roman, then Byzantine followed by the Selçuks, the Armenians, the Mamelukes. In Adana's **Ethnographical Museum**, housed in a former Crusader Church, there is a collection of carpets, weapons, funerary monuments and jewels from the Ottoman period. Amongst the sarcophagi, notice the so-called Achilles sarcophagus, as there is a bas relief depicting the Trojan War. There is also a section given over to statuettes of deities and to Hittite articles.

Only fourteen of the original twenty-one arches remain of the **Tas Koprü**, or the Roman bridge over the river Seyhan, erected by Hadrian in the second century A.D.

The sixteenth-century **Ulu Camii** is a black and white marble mosque. The fine portal of the fifteenth-century Eski Yag mosque is striking. Thirty-five kilometres from Adana, in the hills, is the Castle of Ylan Kale (Castle of the Serpents), a well-preserved Armenian fortress of a massive and mighty appearance with several walls and towers.

The city of Antakya.

ANTAKYA

Antakya, the ancient Antiocheia, and better known as Antioch is twenty-five kilometres from the sea in the province of Hatay. It was built on the banks of the river Orentes (now Asi Nehri) in a fertile plain where fig trees and prickly-pears grow in abundance, and has one of Turkey's more important agricultural export markets. The city is divided into two parts: on the East bank of the river is the old town with Arab-Ottoman buildings and streets and the new town with tall, modern buildings is on the other side of the river.

Antakya was the city where the culture and traditions of Mesopotamia, Phoenicia and Arabia met with Greece and Rome. You can feel the strong Arab connotations which the city has maintained even if it is firmly part of Turkey.

The population, numbering one hundred and fifty thousand, speak Arabic, Turkish and French. The city's cuisine is distinctive, mixing the ingredients of different dishes. Peppers with mint, a typical Arab combination, here accompanies other dishes. Paprika and coriander, spices used in almost all Arab recipes, are also widely used here.

The bazaar in the old part of the town has a classic Arab feel about it. It is a warren of lanes and alleyways, split up according to the different wares. The best things to buy are gold filigree and beautiful silk or woollen shawls.

Antakya is where believers in Christ were for the first time called Christians. The city was originally Graeco-Macedonian, founded by Seleucus I Nicator, a general under Alexander the Great. Under the Roman Empire it

Detail of a Roman mosaic from the Museum of Antakya.

became a centre for intellectuals and was much embellished with monuments. For many years the Byzantines and the Arabs contended for supremacy over Antioch. In 1098 it was taken by the Crusaders and was later destroyed by the Egyptian Mamelukes. In 1516 it became part of the Ottoman Empire and in 1939, after twenty one years under French jurisdiction, once again entered the Turkish republic.

There are not many traces of the past in Antioch today, but the most interesting place is the extensive Museum, situated in the old part of the city. There is a wonderful collection of mosaics made for the houses of the Roman rich. There are statues, and collections of Greek and Roman coins. Stunningly beautiful is the mosaic depicting Oceanus and Thetis surrounded by marine creatures from the depths; so too is the one showing Orpheus Charming the Beasts with his Lyre. One column has an unusual base decorated with a pair of lions; it is Hittite

and dates from the eighth century B.C. There is a splendid Roman sarcophagus in the Museum's garden.

The **Church of St. Peter**, two kilometres out from the centre, was built in a grotto and the facade dates from the time of the Crusades. Inside, part of the mosaic floors survive. Even the **Wood of Daphne** is much visited by tourists, it is still a restful, soothing place with bay trees, fountains and ponds amongst the flower beds and a gentle waterfall. Only eight kilometres from Antioch there is a **mythological park**, at Harbiye. Here the nymph, Daphne, loved and pursued by Apollo, prayed to her father Peneus to turn her into a laurel tree. After that the laurel became the symbol of Apollo. At one time there was a temple here with a statue of Apollo, erected by Seleucus I Nicator.

There is a monastic complex twenty-five kilometres from the city known as the **Monastery of St. Simon**. It is situated in the hills on the road to Samandag, and is formed by the ruins of two monasteries dedicated to St. Simon.

The suggestive pool of Abraham, outside the Halil Rahman mosque at Urfa.

SANLIURFA (HARRAN)

The cities of **Sanliurfa** (now Urfa), the ancient and glorious Edessa, and Harran are places dear to Christians, Jews and Muslims. They are cities without many monuments from the past, but of the past they have the knowledge that they are at the roots of human civilisation. Situated in Northern Mesopotamia, on the borders with Syria, they are arid, dusty and hot but equally fascinating and mysterious. The people are welcoming, and happy to help as guides or to lend a hand. They are a smiling and phlegmatic race. Under the Assyrians the two cities worshipped the Sun and Moon gods. From Harran, Charan in the Bible, Abraham may have departed in search of the promised land in 1850 B.C. Many civilisations prospered in these two cities, from the Assyrians to the Hittites, then Alexander the Great and the Romans who transformed them into military strongholds. Then the Ottomans arrived and absorbed the two cities into the great kingdom.

Today there is hardly any trace of ancient monuments, but every stone, the yellow desert earth and the steppe evoke the story of the beginnings of humanity. The **Halil Rahman Camii** mosque, below the citadel at Urfa, dates from the seventeenth century. It has two domes and the interior is decorated with wooden and stone carving. The mosque is surrounded by a large arched pool known as the **Pool of Abraham**. It is full of carp which are thought to be sacred fishes. Tradition has it that the Patriarch stayed here for a long time. Urfa's archaeological museum has a fine collection of mosaics, inscriptions, panels from the Koran and Haded, Assyrian and Roman artifacts.

There are unusual and fanciful beehive-shaped houses at Harran, made of mud from the local earth which was once fertile. Three **polygonal towers** survive on the fortress which was rebuilt by the Crusaders in the eleventh century on the site of the temple to the Moon goddess Sin.

A Giant's Head at Nemrut Daği.

NEMRUT DAĞI

Nemrut Daği, one of the most suggestive and spectacular sites in Turkey, is actually the name of an enchanted mountain, a legendary place and a genuine attraction for tourists; especially at sunset when everything is imbued in reddish-orange light and the landscape becomes surreal, almost miraculous. Nemrut Daği is part of the Taurus mountain range and, at two thousand five hundred and fifty metres, is the highest point in Northern Mesopotamia.

Today the greatest attraction is owed to the megalomania of King Antiochus I Theos, a descendant of Alexander the Great, who built a magnificent funerary monument for himself and his ancestors on the mountain. Antiochus was one of the kings who ruled over the small Commagene kingdom situated between the Taurus and the valley of the Euphrates. The Commagene kingdom had been originally inhabited in the eighth century B.C. by a semitic race who were replaced by the Assyrians. During the first century B.C. King Mithradates I founded a dynasty, the Commagene, that would last until 72 A.D.

The first-century B.C. tomb of Antiochus I overlooks the terraces on which the sacrarium was constructed. It was made of stone, fifty metres high and with a diameter of one hundred and fifty, but it has been much weathered by time.

On the north terrace are the ruins of the houses of the

Priests, who performed sacrificial rites. There pilgrims met after the journey. At this point there was a monumental gate of which only a stone lion remains proudly guarding Nemrut Daği.

On the west terrace are the stone giant-heads and decorated bas reliefs. The statues, aside from the statue of Antiochus, who was worshipped as a God, represented Graeco-Roman-Persian deities such as Apollo, the Sun God, Zeus and Tyche, the goddess of Fortune. Facing each statue was an altar, used for burning incense to the deity.

On the east terrace are the remains of a **wall** with a few bas reliefs depicting Antiochus I being welcomed by the gods and statues with well-preserved seated figures. At the entrance to the site of Nemrut Daği, there two ten-metre-high columns (originally there were four) at the sides of a **Roman bridge**.

In the two photographs, the stone lion and another Giant's Head at Nemrut Daği.

Diyarbakir, a panorama of the city.

DIYARBAKIR

Diyarbakir, or Amida as it was called under Urartian rule, or Beni Bakir by the nomads is hardly Turkish but Arab. Its inhabitants have called it the Paris of the Orient and it is situated in Eastern Anatolia, in the foothills of the Taurus mountains on the banks of the river Tigris, the Biblical river of Paradise.

Diyarbakir is surrounded by an immense plain growing mostly rice, corn and cotton. Wool is plentiful and fragrant spices are cultivated. Immense sweet, plump watermelons, weighing forty or even sixty kilos grow on the banks of the Tigris, fertilised with pigeon guano. Not surprisingly this city holds an annual watermelon feast.

From Diyarbakir you can float along the Tigris on rafts made of animal skins, the renowned *keler*.

Many civilisations have left their mark on this splendid, unusual city, from the Hurrians in 1,500 B.C., and the Assyrians to the Persians, to Alexander the Great. The Romans conquered here in 115 D.C.; then it was taken by the Sassanids and then by Byzantium. On account of its strategic position it was ceded to the Arabs until 639 A.D., then it again became Selçuk Turkish in 1085 until it joined the Ottoman Empire in 1505. What immediately strikes the visitor on arriving at Diyarbakir are the black basalt **city walls** surrounding the entire city. The walls span six kilometres, they were reinforced by seventy-two towers, and four gates opened into the city. The Harput Kapis gate

A detail of the suggestive and well-preserved walls surrounding the city of Diyarbakir.

at the North, Yenikapi at the East, Mardin Kapisi at the South and Urfa Kapisi (known in medieval times as Bab er-Rum, the Gate of the Romans) at the West.

There are several mosques at Diyarbakir, the most important being the Ulu Cami which dates from 1091. It was built following a terrible earthquake, in perfect Arab style. It has a rectangular floor plan, very like the Moayade mosque in Damascus. It has a fine portal leading to the great courtyard where there are two fountains for ablutions, one of which is under an elegant portico of small columns. Facing the mosque is the old sixteenth-century caravanserai called **Hasan Paşha Hami**. Next to it is the **Archaeological Museum**, in a building which used to be an important Koranic school, the **Zinciriye**

Medresesi, built in the twelfth century.

The **Kasim Padisah Camii**, dating from 1512, is very popular today. The locals say that if you walk around the mosque seven times and touch the minaret, your desire or dream will come true. The minaret, called the "four-legged", indeed is supported by four columns, two metres high. Not far from the Mardin Kapisi Gate is a fine Roman bridge over the river Tigris. It too is made of black basalt and has ten arches.

Before leaving Diyarbakir, visit the famous *grottoes* at the source of the Tigris, called **Iskenderi Birkilin Mağarasi**, meaning the grottos of Alexander the Great. Alexander spent much time here, as did Salmanasser II before him. There are faces of Assyrian kings are carved in the rock.

A panoramic view of Lake Van with the Church of Akdamar. Facing page the Castle of Hosap.

VAN

The city of **Van** is situated at an altitude of 1,750 metres no the shores of the lake which bears the same name. The lake is volcanic and the water so salty that very few fish manage to survive in it. It is large, the opposite shores invisible, and to the eye it looks like the sea. The landscape around is wild and barren. The city, not far from the border with Iran, is enclosed between two rocky extensions, the rock of Van and a craggy hill. In the eleventh century B.C. it was the capital of the Urartian Empire and inhabited by a people who prevented the Assyrians from conquering Anatolia. Van was then taken by the Armenians, the Romans and the Byzantines and in 1387 it was stormed and sacked by Tamerlane. It entered the Ottoman Empire in 1463.

In the old citadel on the rock, along with rock-cut tombs, are the ruins of a medieval fortress built on the site of the Urartian acropolis and the ruins of massive **Urartian ramparts**. There is a rich collection of sculpture and Urartian jewellery in the **Archaeological Museum** as well as Muslim artifacts and a superb array of antique kilim carpets, woven in the area. There are churches and monasteries in the surroundings of Van. **The Church of the Holy Cross**, on the island of Akdamar is a splendid example of well preserved Armenian art. On the exterior of the church, which dates from the tenth century, there are statues and bas reliefs illustrating stories from the Bible.

The **Yedi Kilise monastery**, or the monastery of the seven churches is located on the side of Mount Susan Daği. It was so-called because it encompassed seven churches, one of which was dedicated to the Virgin Mary. The monastery was founded by Armenians at the end of the tenth century and is now in ruins.

A panoramic view of Mount Ararat.

ARARAT

To get to **Mount Ararat**, the famous Biblical mountain, you must first go through Dogubayazit, the most Eastern city in Turkey. **Dogubayazit** is situated on a corn-growing plain at the foothills of the mountain only a few kilometres away from the Iranian and Armenian borders. All around there is yellow wheat, but the landscape is desolate yet fabulous, populated by flocks of sheep and goats looked after by nomads trailing their effects. It is a scene that has remained unchanged for centuries.

In ancient times Dogubayazit was on the caravan route for commerce and trade with the Far East. Here caravans stopped on their way back from China bringing with them silk, chinoiserie and porcelain.

It is situated at an altitude of two thousand metres, and the city and valley are dominated by a fortress-like palace called **Ishak Paşha Sarayi** which rises up like a cathedral in the desert. Building started on the palace in 1685 and it was completed in 1784 by a Kurdish captain Ishak (Isaac) who was governor of the region. The palace is highly unusual, a melange of differing architectural styles, but predominately Persian. It is now in ruins but it once had three hundred and thirty-six rooms and the harem occupied twenty-four of them. There were numerous bathrooms, a mosque and a mausoleum with the tomb of Ishak Paşha, the palace's owner. Close by the palace are the ruins of an ancient Urartian fortress.

An illustration of the impressive Ishak Paşha Saray. On the right, a detail of the Mosque within the Fortress.

From the palace, the view of snow-topped **Mount Ararat** is breathtaking. The mountain is conical in shape, looming and menacing. Its size is such that it has created a strong mystical culture, symbolic of Biblical traditions. For example it has been identified with the point where, at the time of the Flood, humanity was saved with Noah and the Ark. Next to the peak of Great Ararat is the lower summit of Small Ararat, three thousand nine hundred and twenty-five metres high.

Mount Ararat was created by volcanic eruptions in the Quartenary period and it is the highest mountain in Turkey. Many mountaineers have climbed it in search of the lost ark. However the locals are sceptical, even fearful in their relationship with their immense peak.

The Entrance to the Çifte Minare Medresesi, flanked by two splendid minarets.

ERZURUM

Erzurum is situated in the mountains at an altitude of two thousand metres, surrounded by the steppe. It was built on the slopes of Mount Dumlu Daği, the source of the river Euphrates, the biblical river which, with the Tigris, gave birth to human civilisation. The Euphrates meanders across Turkey for nine hundred and seventy kilometres. Erzurum is a city that can take the visitor by surprise - its originality is startling. It is a religious city, but full of contradictions, and it seems split between tradition and modernity, and between conservation and development. It is a frontier city, yet also on the caravan routes; silk merchants stopped here to rest, and both the Russian and Persian borders are close.

Ezurum is a restful, lush city with wide, modern boulevards and parks. There is a local tradition that Erzurum was founded by St. Bartholomew who was journeying to Persia, but the city grew under the Byzantines. The Emperor Theodosius named it Theodosiopolis. Like many others the city suffered repeated invasions from the Armenians and the Arabs who called it Arz ar-Rum, the land of the Romans, which evolved into Erzurum. For a long time the city was controlled by the Selçuk Turks, it

View of the Hatuniye mosque, a mausoleum built in 1255.

was then taken by the Mongolians before passing into the Ottoman Empire in 1451. Christianity took root here early on, when the Armenian king converted and made Christianity the official religion. But no Christian traces have survived as the churches, including the graceful Armenian cathedral, have all been destroyed.

However there are numerous mosques in this religious town. The oldest is the **Ulu Camii**, dating from 1179 which has seven naves and a simply decorated exterior, but the masterpiece of Selçuk architecture is the **Çifte Minare Medresesi**, with splendid majolica-decorated minarets towering over an elegant entrance portal.

It was built as a theological Koran school in 1253 by the Sultan, Alaeddin Keykubad. The **Hatuniye Türbesi** mosque was built as a mausoleum in 1255 by the daughter of the Sultan, Keykubad. This funerary monument has an unusual pyramid roof supporting the dome.

Before leaving the city, do not miss the bazaar where amongst all the modern samovars, antique ones can be found with luck if you look hard.

The other thing to buy here is black amber which the locals use to make rosaries. Superb kilim carpets with unusual designs and colours can also be found at Erzurum.

TRABZON - SUMELA

Trebizond, Trapezus and now **Trabzon** is a wonderful city in North-Eastern Turkey on the Black Sea, with a large harbour built by the Emperor Hadrian. It is an elegant, austere place immersed in luxuriant vegetation, with rivers, lakes and woods which benefit from its rainy climate. Agriculture thrives here and there are crops of tea, tobacco, hemp and flax. The best tea in Turkey, or as the locals would have it, the best tea in the world, grows in Trabzon and in the neighbouring town of Rize, thanks to the continual rain. There are two hundred thousand inhabitants in Trabzon, but this Turkish town is enriched by immigrants from Armenia, Georgia and Russia. Unsurprisingly there are Russian bazaars and flea markets where every kind of thing is bought and sold including excellent Russian caviar, grey, red and black.

Trebizond has an enormously rich heritage, being founded in 750 B.C. by Milesian Greek colonists from Sinope. The Emperor Hadrian added to the town, building fine monuments, and the Apostle Andrew preached here and converted the town to Christianity. Between 1204 and 1461 Trabzon the Splendid was the imperial capital of the Comneni and even after the fall of Constantinople Trabzon remained for many years the last citadel of Graeco-Byzantine civilisation.

There is much to see in Trebizond, and the most important place from an architectonic point of view is the Haghia

The Basilica of Santa Sophia, now the City Museum.
Opposite, a panoramic view of Trabzon, facing the Black Sea.

Sofia, the **Basilica of Santa Sophia**, which is now a museum. It was built on a hill and is surrounded by gardens facing the Black Sea bay. It is a Byzantine church constructed around 1200 A.D. with three naves and a dome supported by four columns. Restoration work in the church has brought back to light its wonderful frescoes and gold Byzantine mosaics that had been plastered over by the Sultan, Mehmet II, when the church was transformed into a mosque.

The **Church of St. Anne**, the oldest in the city, was built during the reign of the Emperor Basil I, right in the centre of the town. It has three naves and a crypt. The four columns separating the naves have Ionic capitals. A beautiful church was dedicated to **Saint Eugenius**, the patron saint of Trabzon who was martyred in the third century; it was erected on the place where his skull was found. The church was constructed on a basilica plan with three naves and three apses and was transformed into a mosque, **Yeni Cuma Camii**, the New Friday mosque. There is a story that the Sultan, Mehmet II, prayed in the Church of St. Eugenius on the Friday that he conquered the city. **Fatih Camii**, a mosque constructed in the former Byzantine basilica with three naves, had a lofty bell tower (replaced by a minaret) known as Panagia Chrysokephalos meaning the Golden-Headed Virgin. It is situated in the Byzantine citadel.

Sumela, forty-five kilometres from Trabzon, possesses a splendid Greek Orthodox monastery dedicated to the

The Greek Orthodox Monastery dedicated to the Virgin Mary, constructed on the mountainside at Sumela. Opposite, the monument to the famous Ottoman architect Sinan, who was born at Kayseri.

Blessed Virgin. It is certainly worth visiting even though it is now mostly in ruins (restoration work is in progress). The monastery is fascinating and ghostly. Looking up at it from below gives the impression that it is floating in space as it was built right on the side of a mountain so dark as to be almost black. An old tradition credits its foundation to two Greek hermits, Barnabas and Sophronius, who were told by the Virgin in a dream to found a monastery in her honour in Pontus.

They reached Sumela in 385, guided by a famous icon of the Virgin. The monastery is known as Meryemana Manastri to the Turks. The remains of the two founding saints are kept in the monastery and pilgrims still come here, but there have been no monks there since 1923 when they moved to Greece.

There is a maze of monastic buildings including the eighteenth-century **church of the Assumption of the Virgin** Mary, the best preserved of the remaining buildings. It has frescoes depicting scenes from the life of Christ and the Virgin and other episodes from the Bible. There is also a fresco illustrating the coronation of Alexius III, the Comneni Emperor, which took place in 1340.

KAYSERI

Kayseri was once an important stop on the caravan trade routes. It is situated at the foot of Erciyas Dag, now an extinct volcano formerly called Mount Argus and has five hundred thousand inhabitants, mostly farmers and weavers. Some of Turkey's most beautiful wool, silk and rayon carpets are made here. Every house has a loom and every street corner has someone selling carpets, or indeed apricots, another of Kayseri's plentiful products. Modern Kayseri with wide streets and large buildings (there has been a building boom in recent years) cohabits with the old city in the citadel which has kept its narrow lanes and alleys and the old colourful and char-

ming Turkish houses, as in old **Bedesten**. There is a bazaar where alongside carpet dealers there are goldsmiths displaying filigree jewellery and cloth merchants with rolls of material. You can buy fine silks, cottons and wool, especially cashmere. Inside the Bedesten there are numerous bistros where you can taste smoked meats coated with red paprika and garlic or delicate melted cheese which is eaten with honey. The flavours create an exquisite combination.

Kayseri, Caesarea in antiquity, was the birthplace of St. Basil the Great (329-379 A.D.), the great bishop of the Orthodox Church and founder of monasticism and its

The Döner Kümbet, or rotating mausoleum, Kayseri's most photographed monument. It was originally the tomb of a princess. Opposite, a typical Cappadocian landscape.

rules that are still practised today. A Father of the Church and a writer, Basil donated his fortune to the poor and founded a monastery that would be a cornerstone of Byzantine culture and, later, a reference point for the Islamic city.

Kayseri's origins go back to the Hittites. Under Rome in 17 A.D. it was renamed Caeserea and a Christian community settled here. The Selçuk overlords added monuments and buildings that are still standing. Before becoming Ottoman in 1515 when it was conquered by Selim, it had been ruled by the Mamelukes.

The **Citadel**, or Hisar, built in the sixth century under Justinian was reconstructed and restored first by the Selçuks and then by the Ottomans. It is surrounded by massive towered walls with two entrance gates. Two car-

ved lions guard the sides of the second gate.

Inside, as well as the small mosque, **Fatih Camii**, there is another mosque, **Honat Hatun Camii** with connecting haman (baths), a Selçuk Koran school (now an **Ethnographical Museum**) and an octagonal mausoleum. The entire complex was erected in 1228 by the Sultan, Alaeddin Keykubad, whose wife was buried in the mausoleum. The **Sehiriye Medredesi**, another Koranic School with an original door dating from 1267 houses a picturesque market selling second-hand books and religious texts. Kayseri's best known and most photographed monument is the **Döner Kümbet**, or rotating mausoleum. It is a decorated cylindrical tower with a conical roof supported on a massive base: a splendid example of Selçuk architecture, built in 1276 as the tomb of a princess.

CAPPADOCIA

Cappadocia is Turkey's most visited area on account of its history, its singularity and the strangeness of its lunar landscape. It is considered to be one of the wonders of the world and for centuries it has sheltered churches, frescoes, mosaics and paintings of Byzantine art.

When the Hittites lived here, Cappadocia covered a larger area but it is now a triangle bordered by the cities of Kayseri, Nevsehir and Nigde in the centre of the Anatolian plateau.

The history of Cappadocia begins with the eruption of two volcanoes, Melendiz Dag near Nigde and Erciyas Dag near Kayseri. Lava covered the entire region changing the landscape.

In the course of millennia rain and wind eroded the tufa creating unusual valleys, fissures, canyons and bizarrely shaped cones. However the terrain was fertile and it was colonised by people who reached it by sea. Dwellings were excavated from the rock and when the first Christians arrived churches and even rough-hewn monasteries were built.

Numerous hermits and ascetics lived in the forgotten valleys. Under the Byzantines who were protectors of those leading religious lives, Cappadocia became a bulwark against attacks by the Arabs, and the population dug out caves and built entire underground cities with massive stone gates to protect themselves.

After the Ottoman conquest these houses in the rock were used as stables and storehouses.

Tufa cones and pyramids, found all over the region of Cappadocia.

ÜRGÜP

From the city of **Ürgüp**, twenty kilometres from Nevsehir and at an altitude of more than one thousand metres, you can see the great valleys of tufa cones and pyramids that give Cappadocia its special character.

Thus Ürgüp is a good base to explore the whole region. The city is small but thriving.

The old houses built with tufa and local stone (some are still decorated) blend in well with the new houses, also built with tufa.

Until a few decades ago, the ten thousand inhabitants of Ürgüp were farmers and shepherds; even today shepherds with their flocks can be seen in the valleys, but with the advance of tourism many have become hoteliers and restaurateurs.

The city is full of small shops and stores selling all kinds of articles from local delicacies to ceramics and small souvenirs of the eye of Allah.

Ürgüp is surrounded by vineyards, wheat fields, orchards and beehives.

The inhabitants who are cheery and prone to laughter claim that Ürgüp's honey is the best in Turkey. During the first few days in June Ürgüp celebrates wine and the grape (the grapes are particularly sweet) by holding a festival which draws people from far and wide to taste wine made in the whole of Cappadocia.

The red wine is hefty and the white rather delicate. Cappadocian grapes have been used to make wine since the practice was started by the Ottomans.

The surreal landscape around Uçhisar.

UÇHISAR

Üçhisar, a village cut from the rock, must be unique. It is a surreal, fantastic landscape of perforated pinnacles and calanques of white ash, with a castle looking down over troglodyte dwellings cut from tufa. From the castle there is a breathtaking view of the region which resembles an enormous white sponge, or a stone forest. Not many people live in Üçhisar.

Walking through the little town, not yet ruined by mass tourism, you feel that time has stopped and that the daily rules and work rhythms arebeing dictated by an unchanging tradition.

Men converse with one another, sitting at precarious tables over glasses of Raki, or cups of tea or coffee. You often come across horse or mule drawn carts on the roads, and the women all cover their heads.

Üçhisar is also called "Pigeon Valley" from its old pigeon-lofts. These are extraordinary monuments resembling the facades of rock-cut churches. Some were excavated and decorated in bright colours so as to attract pigeons as their guano was prized as a fertiliser.

A view of the typically rocky landscape near Göreme. Facing page, a panorama of Uçhisar.

GÖREME

Göreme and its famous valley are situated right in the centre of Cappadocia. Here nature has been overtaken by fantasy; the landscape is made up of valleys large and small, rocky walls, tufa pyramids and cones riddled with holes and odd trees growing in clumps surviving against all odds.

When you see this spectacle, as well as feeling incredulous, you get the sensation that you are in another world, in a lunar landscape. Not by chance it is considered an open-air museum. For centuries it was inhabited by tro-

glodytes carving churches and monasteries out of the rock. It is pleasant, but tiring to go up and down the stairs, into dark passageways and caverns, seeing sanctuaries and houses. Longer trips can be enjoyed on horse or mule-back, without spending large sums of money.

The first Christians came to Göreme to escape from Roman persecutions and they were joined by numerous hermits and ascetics wishing to live in isolation and meditation. They excavated cavities in the rock, burrowed into the mountainside and constructed houses, buildings,

NINE THOUSAND YEARS OF KNOTS

A carpet is essentially precious hand-woven cloth. For the last nine thousand years, or since the neolithic age, in the huge region of Anatolia, women have woven and stitched carpets. This centuries-old tradition has always been practised by women whose houses became complete workshops operating around the loom and the spindle. The secrets and skills were handed down from mother to daughter.

Because of nomadic traditions, Turkey - and the Turks make this claim themselves - was probably the inventor of the carpet, and its designs and styles later mixed with those of other places such as Persia.

in Istanbul entire shops and stores are crammed with carpets of every size, old and modern, from all over the country.

Bursa, not far from Istanbul, produces beautiful carpets, almost exclusively of silk called Hereke. They are exquisitely made with more than a million knots per square metre. They usually have floral designs of roses or carnations. In the past these carpets were used as precious adjuncts to mosques or the sultan's palace. The floral and animal motifs found on silk carpets from Kayseri (Caesarea, the ancient capital of Cappadocia) allude to paradise, the Garden of Eden.

Carpets made in Bergama are woollen with red geometric designs. Milas and Kars carpets are also made of wool, but their colours vary from yellow to tobacco, from light to dark

Examples of Turkey's marvellous carpets. Above a display of wares made at Uçhisar. Above left, a woman at work on a loom.

The dominant colour in Turkish carpets, whether the dye is vegetable or chemical, is red which symbolises wealth. Green is the colour of paradise and blue the colour of grandeur and nobility. Yellow has always represented protection from misfortune and black stands for problems that have been solved. Carpets can be made of wool, silk or cotton or of mixed fibres. In Anatolia wool always means the fleece of sheep, goat or dromedary. The traditional Turkish tying knot, or node, is called Ghiordes from the place with the same name in Anatolia, but it is not the only one.

Tourists wishing to buy a Turkish carpet are embarrassed for choice. In the Grand Bazaar

brown. Kulas and Husaks and those made in Smyrna have a long tradition and have long been exported to the West to decorate churches and royal palaces. They have sober, refined colours. A safe investment is a Taban carpet made in Konya with pastel colours, woollen knots and cotton wefts.

Even Marco Polo was enchanted by Taban carpets, and they are much in demand in the West, but they are not easy to find. Finally Kilim carpets are woven without knots, according to a tradition that dates back to neolithic times. These carpets have the greatest religious and mythological symbolism; they were called, not by chance, the carpets of the gods.

Rock-cut churches in the Valley of Göreme.

stables, mills, churches and monasteries that were invisible from the outside, but inside their dwellings were functional and well laid out.

Their churches and monasteries were later adorned with frescoes, paintings and icons. In the Göreme valley alone there are more than a thousand churches and monasteries, the earliest dating from the seventh century. An ancient local tradition claims that the monks managed to create three hundred and sixty-five churches in a single year, at a rate of one a day.

Under the Byzantines, during the iconoclastic period, work on decorating the churches was suspended and the monks were persecuted. Their goods were confiscated and many monasteries were forced to close.

Only around 843 A.D., after the victory of the iconolaters (worshippers of images) were the monks able to return and vigorously set about building and decorating more churches and monasteries, and religious architecture once again flourished in the valley.

The **Tokali Kilise**, or the Church of the Buckle is the largest and most important church in Göreme and indeed in Cappadocia and the lavishness of its decorations and frescoes has survived to this day. At one time this church housed a precious collection of gold and jewels, including a large gold buckle (hence the name of the church), which later disappeared mysteriously. The frescoes in the church date from the tenth century and they are predominately blue in colour. They narrate, in chronological

Wall paintings in the romantic Karanlik Kilise at Göreme. Opposite page, tourists admiring the open air museum.

order, episodes from the life of Christ, from the Annunciation to the Ascension into heaven. Other decorations record the life of Basil the Great, the Bishop-Patron Saint of Cappadocia. The structure of the church is different from the others, having a transverse nave and an atrium formed from the interior of an earlier church, called the Old Church which originally had a single aisle and a vaulted roof.

The **Karanlik Kilise**, or Dark Church is so called because of its lack of light, having only one small aperture opening on to the narthex which provides hardly any. This has meant that its frescoes have kept their brilliant colours and luminosity. Entrance to the church is via a staircase. It was built in the eleventh century on two storeys and was once part of a monastery; there is still a refectory with a table and benches for the monks and a dormitory excavated in the rock.

The central dome of the Karanlik Kilise is decorated with a splendid image of Christ Pantocrator and rests on columns whose lower parts are embellished. Blue is the predominant colour of the frescoes which illustrate the Crucifixion and Christ's Last Supper. The **Çarikli Kilise**, the Church of the Sandal, was so named because of footprints found in the entrance in front of the door. Legend has it that they were the footprints of Jesus Christ, who appeared there after the Resurrection. This church too is richly decorated with paintings showing episodes from the life of Christ: one fresco showing the betrayal of Judas above the arch on the left door is particularly beautiful. The unusual feature of the Carikli Kilise is that it was excavated from the same rock as Karanlik Kilise and the two churches have facing entrances.

TEA AND COFFEE: RITUAL AND TRADITION

Tea, or cay, is the real national drink.
In Turkey tea is grown on plantations at Rize, a city near the Black Sea with heavy rainfall in winter. It is the colour of mahogany and it should by unclouded and crystal clear. It is served in small tulip-shaped glasses.
In shops, peoples' houses and in the streets, you are almost always offered tea, even apple tea or tea flavoured with bergamot, a fruit which grows copiously in Mediterranean Turkey. Coffee was introduced into Turkey by the Arabs and it is served at the end of a meal. Turkish coffee is a genuine ritual.
It is prepared in a small coffee pot with a long handle, called "cezve", and made with finely ground toasted coffee beans, and drunk in tiny cups.
In addition the Turks like to foretell the future by inspecting the grounds left at the bottom of their cups.

A panorama of the evocative ravine with tufa cones in the area of Zelve.
On the following two pages, a detail from the frescoes in one of the rock-cut churches and a triple tufa cone at Paşabag.

ZELVE

Not far from Avanos is the city of **Zelve** situated in the strangest valley with ravines, high rocks and tufa cones - one the most beautiful, perfect places in Cappadocia.

Zelve is a rock city concealed in the valley and it was lived in until thirty years ago. It is surrounded by vineyards and sunflowers but above all it is a bird paradise where birds of all species flock together, hiding in apertures in the old houses where they make their nests.

The inhabitants lived in dwellings excavated from the rock but continuous erosion in the area weakened the walls of their houses forcing them to abandon the town, and they moved to a new village called Yeni Zelve.

At Zelve and in the whole valley lived numerous communities of monks, hermits, and ascetics seeking isolation, but not many of their churches and sanctuaries constructed in the rocks have survived and they are mostly in poor condition. The importance and fascination of these churches lay in their wall paintings, the oldest in Cappadocia. These are important for their iconography, depicting with extreme simplicity and primitiveness the symbols of Christianity, the religion that was taking root. The most common subjects were the Cross, the symbol of the passion, or a fish which stood in Greek letters (ichthys) for Jesus Christ, Son of God, Saviour.

In the **Balikli Kilise**, also known as the Church of the Fish, there are numerous wall paintings depicting fishes and the ceiling is decorated with a great Cross with fishes at the side.

In the **Üzümlü Kilise**, or Church of the Grapes, there are wall paintings with vines and bunches of grapes as wine in Christianity is the symbol of the Eucharist.

There are several wall painting illustrating deer, the Cross and fish in the **Geykli Kilise**, the Church of the Deer.

As well as the churches at Zelve to see, there are ancient presses and stone mills that have survived over the centuries in spite of the geological faults in the area.

The "Fairies' Chimneys", the original and unmistakable tufa cones ten metres high from the Valley of Pasabag.

THE FAIRIES' CHIMNEYS

Close to Zelve is the Valley of Pasabagi, or the Valley of the Monks, but for the Turks, **the fairies' chimneys**. The landscape here too is startling, with perfectly formed tufa cones ten metres high grouped together and others standing in isolation. Clusters of these pinnacles are covered by unmistakable black caps, rather like a monk's hood, which have protected them from rain and erosion. There are fruit trees all around, mostly apples and figs which have grown spontaneously and neat rows of vines laden with grapes.

The local people who worked the land believed that wicked fairies and elves lived in these "chimneys", ready to cast evil spells.

Pasabagi is also known as the valley of the monks because monks and hermits came from all over to make their own dwellings, as they did elsewhere in Cappadocia, because its strange landscape encouraged solitude and meditation.

St. Simeon was one of the anchorites who chose this valley, according to tradition. He lived on a cone, an outcrop of tufa, praying, healing the sick and even advising the powerful.

The so-called **Chapel of St. Simeon** can be visited in small groups. The paintings in the interior date from the tenth century but they are in poor condition and some have completely vanished.

On the back wall of the church there are frescoes with scenes from the life of the saint; one fresco showing the saint with his mother is particularly expressive.

A display of ceramics from Avanos, a small artisan city of potters and weavers.

AVANOS

Avanos is a small Cappadocian city of artisans. It is situated on the banks of the river Kizilirmak, the "Red River", Turkey's longest river which the Hittites named Marassantiya two thousand five hundred years before Christ. The water is coloured by red clay deposits used to make Avanos's famous pottery. Every year in the summer Avanos and its artisans celebrate with a festival where the finest ceramics are displayed. There are songs and dances in traditional costumes, wine and gastronomical treats in profusion. The streets of ancient Avanos are lined with square white houses with wooden balconies on small terraces. Inside the town the streets give way to workshops and the road surfaces are covered with vases, amphoras, earthenware pots in varying sizes, mugs and plates. Other artisans in Avanos are involved in weaving carpets and Avanos is a good place to buy. There is a weaving school in the city, perhaps the only one in Turkey, teaching apprentices the ancient arts of weaving and dyeing the wool and silks, and preventing the traditions of this ancient art from dying out. In the centre of the town there is an unusual monument figuring two women kneeling at a loom and a potter at work.

Avanos was the ancient city of Venasa and the inhabitants worshipped the eagle, the incarnation of the God Zeus. The Selçuks erected numerous religious buildings. The private houses at Avanos, where the interior rooms give on to interior courtyards without communicating with one another, date from the Ottoman period.

The Church of Takkeli.

SOĞANLI

Soğanli and its valley were lived in by monks and hermits, like the Göreme and Peristrema valleys, and it too is rich in churches and dwellings carved out of the tufa rock, but here they resemble flawed pyramids and sieve-like calanques riddled with holes. The locals used these as nests or dovecotes for pigeons, as they used pigeon guano as a fertiliser. To get this far is bordering on the adventurous, but it repays the effort. As well as the unforgettable landscapes, you can carry away a solid souvenir, the locally made rag dolls, or the amazingly-coloured and elegantly-made handsome puppets.

Walking up the stream that runs through Soğanli, you come to the **Gök Kilise**, or the Church of the Sky. It has two naves which join in the apse and there are frescoes, but they are no longer distinguishable.

There is a fresco illustrating St. George slaying a dragon which looks like a giant snake in the Yilanli Kilise. Unfortunately the other frescoes are indecipherable.

The **Kubbeli Kilise** is really three interconnecting chapels. The first, called **Sakli Kilise**, is hidden alongside the other two which were built on top of one another.

The latter two chapels were once richly decorated with frescoes dating from the ninth century, but regrettably they are now mostly faded, but faint traces can be seen. The church is surmounted by excavated domes; Kubbe is indeed the word for a dome.

The ancient underground city of Kaymakli.

DERINKUYU-KAYMAKLI

Seven kilometres separate **Kaymakli** from **Derinkuyu**, the two underground cities that may have been connected by a long passageway in antiquity.

In Cappadocia alone there are about thirty-five underground cities: some have been restored, others have yet to be discovered, and others still await restoration. Kaymakli is located deep down in a grotto below a hill made of soft tufa that had once been used by the Romans as a cemetery. Once you have descended down into the interior, you are met with a labyrinthine maze of corridors, passages, wells and rooms both above and beneath you. It is a dank, chilly place but not without magic and adventure and it is not unlike the catacombs in Rome. There are signposts showing the way and they help you not to get lost, which would be all too easy. These underground cities were Christian oases, and date from the second century A.D. and they were completed between the sixth and the tenth centuries. They were initially built as safe havens from Roman persecutions and later offered protection from Arab attacks. Kaymakli is constructed on eight different levels and lies forty-five metres deep, but Derinkuyu, the other underground city whose name means 'deep well' is a great deal larger, spreading over twelve levels and reaching a depth of one hundred and twenty metres.

Inside these two sites lived entire communities of Christians who worked there, living alongside their livestock and they built small churches with altars and crosses, and cemeteries for the burial of the dead. In between the galleries seemed like streets, with intersecting corridors with rudimentary shafts for air and light. These underground cities could be sealed off using enormous stone wheels measuring a metre and a half in diameter.

THE VALLEY OF IHLARA

Ihlara is a large village on the banks of the Melendiz Dere, the river that flows through high rocky peaks, similar to a canyon. It was formerly known as the valley of Peristrema, and was a favoured place for retreat amongst the Byzantine monks. Rather as at Göreme monks built monasteries, churches and hermitages by digging them out of the rock. Its artistic heritage has been much damaged, but it was just as grand as the Göreme valley and the spirit of the dawn of Christianity is perhaps here more keenly perceived.

The Peristrema valley runs from the village of Seline to the village of Ihlara, a distance of thirteen kilometres, the final destination of this excursion, and the path is desolate and barren except for the trees which grow near the river. It is an unsettling place, but at the same time captivating on account of its strange nature. It takes three hours to walk the whole distance along the paths and it is much less tiring, as well as being more romantic to hire a horse or a mule from one of the locals.

A tour of the valley of the churches begins by descending an iron staircase. The first church you come to on the left bank is the **Alti Kilisesi**, also known as the Church under

A detail from the frescoes of one of the numerous churches in the Ihlara Valley. Facing page, a panorama of the valley.

the Tree, built on the plan of a Greek cross.

On the opposite bank is the Serpents' Church, the **Yilani Kilise** which still has splendid frescoes; notice the fresco of Christ the Judge flanked by two Angels and the fresco illustrating the Forty Martyrs of Sebaste which was an Armenian metropolis when the fresco was painted, but is now Sivas, a Turkish town.

The forty martyrs were Christian soldiers condemned to death by the Roman Licinius. This church possesses the only example in Cappadocia of a fresco illustrating the Weighing of the Souls (psychostasy). The church takes its name from a painting of an alarming three-headed serpent. The **Karagedik Kilisesi**, or the Church of the Black Collar has been badly damaged but there are still frescoes with scenes from the life of Christ and the Virgin Mary, in chronological order, to be seen in the

Korar Kilise, also known as the Perfumed Church.

On the other bank, the left side, not far from the village of Belisirima is the fine church dedicated to St. George, the **Kirk Dam Alti Kilisesi**, with paintings dating from the twelfth century.

There is a detail in a fresco painted on the ceiling showing the figure of a richly-dressed emir in the act of making a presentation next to St. George.

The **Direkli Kilise** or Church of the Columns has three apses and frescoes depicting the lives of saints and their martyrdoms.

The **Baktin Kilise** is a small single-aisled church and its frescoes are faded and indistinct, but what has survived is sufficient for the visitor to perceive the elegance of the figures of Christ and the Virgin Mary, executed in a simple manner before the onset of iconoclasm.

NEVŞEHIR

Nevşehir is a peaceful, modern city on the Anatolian plateau where the calanques of white volcanic ash and lunar landscapes are curiously absent. Fifty thousand people live there in the shadow of a citadel which dates from the Selçuk period with a Byzantine fortress. The city of Nevşehir has converted to tourism and provides most services, and almost anything can be purchased. It is an ideal starting-off point to explore the entire Cappadocian region.

The people are hospitable and well-disposed towards visitors, happily inviting them into their homes and offering them tea with fresh or dried fruit. Notwithstanding tourism in Cappadocia, more than any other part of Turkey, the people have kept their ancient souls of Asiatic civilisations: patriarchal, nomadic and rustic.

In ancient times Nevsehir was known to the Hittites, who may also have founded the city which was to experience many different civilisations during its history. A sea-faring population who came from the Aegean colonised it in the thirteenth century B.C., and it was later conquered by Cimmerians, Assyrians, Persians and then again by the Greeks before becoming part of the Roman Empire in 17 A.D. For a long time it was under Byzantine rule, then taken by Selçuk nobles who were well known for their religious and political tolerance. In fact Christians were never persecuted under their rule.

The twelfth and thirteenth centuries were the most productive in Cappadocia, when numerous monasteries were

A group of women wearing traditional Cappadocian costumes. Below, colour and fruit from Nevsehir.

constructed and embellished.

The view from the old citadel, a Byzantine fortress restored both by the Selçuks and the Ottomans, is phenomenal. The narrow alleys of old houses are crammed with small shops and stalls. On the street corners, women with their heads covered crouch on small stools selling, on improvised counters, beautiful lace, covers and crochet curtains at fair prices.

The **Nevşehirli Paşha Kulliyesi** is a complex of religious buildings with a Koranic School, a haman, a library, a university and a mosque which is still in use.

The city has a small **museum** with objects dating from the Hittite, Phrygian, Roman, Byzantine and Ottoman periods discovered during excavations. There is a collection of utensils for daily use, vases, costumes and jewels.

The Lion Gate at the entrance to the city.

BOGAZKALE

Bogazkale, formerly **Boğaz-köy**, and Hattusa in anti-quity, is a small town with an important history, being the capital of the Hittite kingdom. Hattusa had been inhabited in the palaeolithic period, but its history really begins with the Hittites. Its ruins are amongst Turkey's most original and striking with a circle of walls six kilometres long constructed on the ridge of a hill. Today Hattusa is an agricultural village of almost three thousand souls that has recently discovered tourism, and every year more and more visitors come.

Hittites are mentioned both in the Odyssey and the Old Testament, and they were an Indo-European race who originated in the Caucasus, and who called themselves 'nesites' from the name of the city of Nesa. In around 2,300 B.C. they settled in Anatolia where they founded city states and traded in iron, more precious than gold at that time. At the height of their grandeur and economic power in 1,600 B.C. the Hittites conquered Babylon.

Their decline was precipitated by the arrival of sea-faring peoples from Europe. The Empire disintegrated into numerous small states, like Hetei, a part of Syria today, or Ephron, the Hittite city renamed Hebron where, in the Book of Genesis, Abraham bought a cave where he buried his wife Sarah. Hattusa became the Hittite capital and King Hattusili I erected the first city walls and enriched the city with buildings and monuments.

During the fourteenth century B.C. Hattusa was besieged and burnt on several occasions. It was reconstructed by the Phrygians and later conquered by the Persians. By the

time of the Romans little more than a village remained.

The walls surrounding the city are well preserved and date from 1,400 B.C. and wind through the rocks for over six kilometres. Hattusa had four gates of which ruins remain and the grandest was the **Lion Gate**, the most important Hittite monument, with had two fine sculpted stone lions projecting from the outer side.

The **Kralkapi** or King's Gate was so called because it possessed a relief depicting a regal male figure, which turned out, however, to be a representation of a Hittite War God who was the city's protector. The relief is now in the museum at Ankara. At one time the gate was flanked by two massive towers.

The King's residence was in the great fortress called the **Büyükkale**. In 1906 a clay tablet was found in one of the rooms in the palace. It had an cuneiform inscription with the terms of a treaty between King Hattusili III and the Egyptian Pharoah, Ramesses II.

Only the foundations and stone ruins remain of the five temples that once characterised Hattusa. The best known, and the largest was the **Great Temple**, the Buyuk Mabed, dedicated to the Weather God and built around the fourteenth century. During excavations tablets and fragments of writing in cuneiform were found in the interior and they are now kept in the Ankara museum. They have proved to be most valuable for historians and scholars of language in reconstructing the history of the Hittite civilisation. The temple was really a proper citadel. There were water cisterns, storerooms (numerous amphoras, water-jars and earthenware containers for storing wheat have been found inside), as well as, naturally, altars where sacred rites to the deity were performed.

The Hittite rock sanctuary.

YAZILIKAYA

Two kilometres from the city of Bogazskoy is the Hittite rock shrine of **Yazilikaya** which means Inscribed Rock in Turkish. The **Hittite pantheon** was excavated from the valley slopes and possesses important sculpted reliefs. There were two great chambers facing the temple where sacrificial rites were performed. In the first chamber there is a relief depicting a long procession of deities, female goddesses on the right, gods on the left. The second room was perhaps a burial chamber and it contains a series of bas reliefs and a frieze depicting the twelve mountain gods, also known as the "blessed twelve". In front of you is a bas relief figuring king Tudhaliya IV being embraced by the god Sharuma. The most figurative frieze depicts the more important deities. The **Sun Goddess Hepatu** stands astride a panther next to Teshub, the Weather God, who rules over all the gods of the mountain. There were numerous deities, as the Hittites venerated more than a thousand gods.

Hittite archeological ruines.

ALACAHÖYÜK

A further Hittite archaeological site can be seen at **Alacahöyük**, an agricultural village twenty-five kilometres from Bogazkoy. It is smaller than Yazilikaya and the greater part of its monuments and originals friezes were moved to the Anatolian Civilisations Museum at Ankara so only reproductions can be seen at the site.

The importance of this site derives from the fact that it was inhabited by 4,000 B.C. Its most important monument is the **Sphinx Gate** which was the gateway to a temple. The Sphinxes, creatures of Egyptian mythology, were located with their heads facing the city.

On one of the gates there is an double-headed eagle, clutching a hare in her claws.

Not far from the monumental gate are the ruins of a **necropolis** and the small museum of Alacahöyük is next to the site. It has a collection of objects dating from 5,000 B.C. to the bronze age and some articles of Phrygian origin.

ANKARA

Before being proclaimed the new capital of Turkey in 1924 by Mustafa Kemal Atatürk, **Ankara**, Angora or Ancyra was a modest township, almost heathland in the middle of the Anatolian steppe, and it had nothing of the glory or power of Istanbul under the Sultans.

Today the steppe and the surrounding plateau are still there but Ankara has become a fine European city with almost four million inhabitants, situated at an altitude of eight hundred and fifty metres.

Ankara has wide streets and large squares, and tall, modern buildings. There are sumptuous villas, mostly in the embassy quarter, leafy trees, gardens and a large park, the Cenclik Parki. When Atatürk settled here, he ordered trees to be planted in quantity and areas of greenery created so as to transform the city's barren and arid appearance.

Thus Ankara is a new city, the city of Atatürk, with rhythms stemming from politics, government and parliament. It is a city of ministries, embassies, offices and universities, commercial centres and shops, some even selling antiques. It is the city where the country's changes have been swiftest and more profound, even though traditions have been respected. There is, therefore, a division between the suburbs where the houses are coloured modern cubes, the residential quarters and old Ankara, with its citadel dominated by the Byzantine fortress Ak Kale where there are narrow streets and sharply ascending alleys; wooden houses with blue stucco facades, and restaurants, mostly frequented by tourists, where in the kitchens women with their heads bowed and covered prepare pastry for traditional

Panorama of Ankara.

ravioli called Manti (stuffed with minced meat) served with yoghurt and tomato sauce, on low Turkish tables.

Notwithstanding the vitality, modernity and cosmopolitan air brought by the numerous foreign residents and contact with many different cultures, Ankara lacks the charm and fascination of Istanbul and in particular, its spirit which has nothing to do with the absence of ancient monuments.

Even so Ankara has a long history and saw many civilisations starting with the Hittites, the ancient Indo-European race mentioned in the Old Testament, who settled here in 2,300 B.C.

Hittites were the first people to use chariots in warfare. Then the Phrygians arrived from the Aegean Sea, followed by the Persians, Alexander the Great and the Seleucids. In 250 B.C. it fell into the hands of the tribe of the Galatians until in 25 B.C. Caesar Augustus brought the city into the great Roman Empire, renaming it Ancyra and it became the capital of Galatia. The Emperor Nero enlarged Ancyra adding numerous buildings and monuments. Ancyra became a Christian city early on and a place where St. Peter preached the gospel for some years. Two important Councils of the Church were held here in 314 A.D. and in 358 A.D.

After the Byzantine period, the Arabs invaded. After 1101 it was governed by the Selçuks, and at the time of the Crusades it became part of the Ottoman Empire.

The **Arslanhane Camii**, Ankara'a oldest mosque dates from 1289; its name means the Animal Mosque and there are two large Roman stone lions in the courtyard. It is a Selçuk mosque and was built using materials and fragments from different architectural periods. There are five naves and a stupendous wooden roof; the mimber too is wooden, but the mihrab is decorated with tiled mosaic.

The **Column of Julian**, known by the locals as the Minaret of the Queen of Sheba, is fifteen metres high and it was dedicated to the Emperor Julian the Apostate in 362, after he had visited the city. The **Hacii Bayram Camii** is a fifteenth-century mosque gives on to a large square where people sit happily at tables. This mosque houses the tomb of Haci Bayram and is a place of pilgrimage for Muslims; it is also the place where the ancient religious rite of circumcision is performed. Children come here, accompanied by their parents, dressed in colourful clothes and wearing a special cloak bordered in synthetic fur.

Another unusual feature of this mosque is that it shares a wall with the ruins of the **Temple of Augustus.** Inscribed on temple walls, in both Latin and Greek, is the "Monumentum Ancyranum", recording the achievements, the Res Gestae, of Augustus, in fact, his political testament. It was built around 20 B.C. on the site of a shrine dedicated to the Phrygian god Men, but it is currently covered in scaffolding while restoration works are carried out.

Only the foundations and the pool remain of the third-century Roman Baths. Many pieces of broken sculpture

A portrait of Atatürk.
Below, the Kocatepe Mosque, the largest in the city. It was built between 1967 and 1987. Facing page, Atatürk's Mausoleum.

and tomb fragments can be seen in the palaestra.

The **Anatolian Civilisations Museum** is one of the most important museums in Turkey. Its valuable collection encompasses the story of all the various civilisations established in Asia Minor. It is housed in two separate buildings, one in the old Bedesten, and the other in a former caravanserai, below the citadel. The artifacts on display come from excavations that have taken place in various Turkish cities. The exhibits are displayed chronologically, beginning with a collection of stone utensils for daily use dating from the palaeolithic age and semi-precious jewels from the sixth millennium. There are rare and beautiful statues of the Mother Goddess, stone lions, vases, and terracotta animals. One of the exceptional exhibits is a Hittite earthenware tablet bearing a cuneiform description of a sacrificial ceremony. Next there is a collection of Urartian bronze shields, stone reliefs, a bronze cauldron and numerous ivory statuettes. The Urartians were an agricultural race that had settled by Lake Van. There are, of course, Greek and Roman objects, such as a fine bust of the Emperor Trajan, and a collection of Roman, Selçuk and Ottoman coins.

The **Mausoleum of Atatürk**, situated on the summit of a hill, is a place of civic veneration since Atatürk was much loved by the people who considered him to be the father of the Turks and the Republic. It was built between 1944 and 1953 and is situated at the top of a wide boulevard.

There is a vast open space in front of the mausoleum, reflecting the grandeur of the structure itself. On either side there are colonnaded galleries and the interior houses museums where even the smallest items belonging to Atatürk have been kept: photographs, pens, shaving equipment, even his motorcar.

The ceremony of the Changing of the Guard, in front of the mausoleum, is evocative, as is watching the queues of children, hushed by their teachers, who enter the mausoleum clutching the Turkish flag - white star and sickle on a red background. A staircase leads to the mausoleum proper, which is in the form of a temple, constructed entirely in black and white-veined green marble with a ceiling covered in gold mosaics. The impressive bronze doors were made in Italy. The funerary monument itself is marble, but the remains of the blue-eyed General repose in an underground crypt.

INDEX